NAZI GERMANY

A CRITICAL INTRODUCTION

MARTIN KITCHEN

TEMPUS

First published 2004

Tempus Publishing Limited
The Mill, Brimscombe Port,
Stroud, Gloucestershire, GL5 2QG
www.tempus-publishing.com

British Library Cataloguing in Publication Data.
A catalogue record for this book is available from the British Library.

ISBN 0 7524 2341 X

Typesetting and origination by Tempus Publishing Limited
Printed and bound in Great Britain

CONTENTS

one
GERMANY, HITLER AND THE ORIGINS OF THE NSDAP
20 April 1889–30 January 1933

INTRODUCTION

How could it possibly have happened? Many a contemporary asked this question in desperation and, many decades later, with tens of thousands of meticulous studies of every aspect of the Third Reich, the answer still eludes us. How could a highly educated, cultured and technically advanced society with a long tradition of the rule of law idolize an ill-educated beer-hall demagogue, a venomous racist, a bigoted philistine, and a sadistic monomaniac? How could a country, which had made such an unsurpassed contribution to European civilization, devote its exceptional skills and energies to a brutal and senseless war of conquest and industrialized mass-murder on a scale that still beggars the imagination?

It is indeed a baffling story. Adolf Hitler was a complete nonentity until the age of thirty. Then for the next 26 years his impact on history was unequalled and indelible. Germany and Germany's victims are still trauma-tized by his regime, and the wounds that National Socialism opened may never heal.

In the summer of 1932 most political observers were convinced that Hitler's meteoric rise was a spent force. Support for the party dropped dramatically, President Hindenburg refused to appoint him chancellor, and the Nazi movement was rent with dissension. Yet within a few weeks he had been appointed chancellor and contemporaries were dazed by the speed of the 'national revolution'. Within six months the National Socialists had destroyed all other political parties, the trades unions, and every asso-ciation and club whether of the left or the right. The federal system had been virtually dismantled, local government was firmly in the hands of the party, political opponents real or imagined had been driven out of the civil service, the press muzzled and Germany's estimable Jewish community was submitted to vicious discrimination and shameful indignities. The Big Bad Wolf huffed and puffed and blew the house down with remarkable ease.

The causes of this disaster are highly complex and deeply embedded in German history. It was not a singular event, an accident, an exception, or a political Chernobyl as historians such as Friedrich Meinecke, Gerhard Ritter and Eberhard Jaeckl have argued. Nor did Auschwitz blot out all previous German history, as Jürgen Habermas would have us believe. The Third Reich was not the inevitable outcome of the course of German history from Luther through Frederick the Great to Bismarck and Hindenburg as proponents of the 'special development' (*Sonderweg*) theory insist. This latter view is as simplistic as the traditional Prussian-conservative view of German history as reaching its apotheosis in the unification of Germany in 1871; a process that many nationalists felt was completed by Hitler in 1938 with the *Anschluss* of Austria.

This positive and Hegelian view of Germany's historical development was first turned on its head by Edmond Vermeil. He argued that Germany was on the wrong track from the time of the Hohenstaufens with their campaigns in Italy in the twelfth century (a view shared for very different reasons by the nationalist historians of the nineteenth century). A.J.P. Taylor and William Shirer put the blame on Martin Luther and Prussian militarism. Somewhat later, Hans-Ulrich Wehler posed the question why it was that Germany did not develop into a liberal democratic society on the British model.

On closer examination the *Sonderweg* explains precious little. Every country has its *Sonderweg* in certain respects, and German economic development, social structure and conflicts, and the opposition of established élites to liberal reform differed little from the experience in Britain or France. Furthermore, the concept of continuity, which comes from the cinema, is profoundly unhistorical in that it results from reading history backwards so that the contingent appears inevitable.

The forces of Ferdinand Braudel's *longue durée* certainly played their part in aiding the rise of National Socialism, but more immediate circumstances were far more important: a lost war and a harsh peace settlement, runaway inflation in 1923 and the long depression that began in 1928, mass unemployment, a perceived communist threat, the collapse of the democratic political system, and above all the roles of the individual actors with their intrigues and grievous errors of judgement. The Republic collapsed, the authoritarian conservative forces were at a loss as to what should be done and the National Socialists seized the opportunity offered by this economic, political and social crisis. The immediate outcome was not inevitable, but it is comprehensible. What happened subsequently is altogether another matter. Historians are neither judge nor jury, but to comprehend in no sense means to condone, and we shall never understand enough about the Nazi dictatorship to be able to forgive. Historical understanding stands mute before the horror of the Shoah; all attempts at explanation are condemned to be facile, glib and impious. It is right and proper that, confronted with this ultimate negation of civilization, the human intellect and imagination should remain painfully baffled.

HITLER AND THE NSDAP: THE EARLY YEARS

Every schoolchild learnt in their National Socialist catechism that: 'Our *Führer* Adolf Hitler was born in Braunau on the Inn on 20 April 1889. His father was an Austrian customs officer, his mother a housewife.' The details of his childhood and youth are shrouded in myth, partly of his own making in *Mein Kampf* and partly from the recollections of his boyhood friend August Kubizek. Suffice it to say he was brought up in a respectable *petit-bourgeois* milieu and even after his father's death in 1903 he was not lacking in material support.

He left school after the ninth year and led an idle semi-bohemian existence first with his mother in Linz until 1907 and then in Vienna. He made two abortive attempts to enrol in the Vienna Academy for Fine Arts, but the examining committee felt that he had little talent as an artist. He stayed in Vienna until 1913, making a modest living selling hand-painted postcards of the city and going to the opera at every possible opportunity.

Pre-war Vienna was a hotbed of political anti-Semitism. Georg Ritter von Schönerer was an old man in 1907, his influence waning, but Hitler was to echo many of his ideas. Schönerer despised democracy and preached anti-Semitism and 'National Socialism', by which he meant an attack on big business and liberal capitalism combined with social reform and help for the small farmers and artisans. He insisted on being addressed as *Führer* (leader) and used the *Heil!* greeting. His followers were mostly vegetarians and teetotallers. In later years Hitler was to criticize him for failing to see the need for mass support and for his attacks on the Catholic Church.

8

Karl Lueger, the popular mayor of Vienna at the time of Hitler's arrival in the city, also ran on an anti-Semitic ticket. Unlike Schönerer, he was a rabble-rouser who courted a mass following among small businessmen and artisans, the butchers, bakers and candlestick makers who were threatened by modern capitalism. Hitler's main regret was that Lueger's anti-Semitism, although often crude and vicious, was regrettably unprincipled. He had a number of Jewish friends and acquaintances, and when challenged on this point made the famous remark: 'I decide who is a Jew'.

On the wilder shores of anti-Semitism, the mad former Cistercian monk and phoney aristocrat Lanz von Liebenfels preached a primitive racism in the pages of his newspaper *Ostara*. He had a vision of the blue-eyed blond 'Aryan' race locked in battle against black animals. The inferior races were to be sterilized and even exterminated so that pure Aryan blood could be preserved. Lanz also adopted the swastika as a symbol.

Much of this was merely coffee-shop twaddle, typical of the Vienna of the day, but such ideas had a profound influence on young Hitler. As Karl Kraus was to point out, only when Austrian madness was harnessed to Prussian efficiency did it become deadly. Hitler and his followers took over a modern state and instead of ending their days as taproom bores or inmates of congenial psychiatric institutions, they were able to indulge in their crazed fantasies and thus inflict untold suffering on the world.

In 1913 Hitler moved to Munich in order to avoid military service in the Austrian Army. He was in Munich when war broke out and immediately enlisted in the Bavarian Army. He was an obedient and courageous soldier, serving as a runner between regimental headquarters and the front line. His commanding officer commented that he showed absolutely no leadership qualities and he never rose above the rank of corporal. Hitler the maladroit loner was profoundly affected by the war experience: by the 'socialism of field grey', the rigid discipline, the sense of national mission, and the belief that life was an endless battle. Struggle (*Kampf*) was to become the key word in the National Socialist vocabulary.

Hitler was in hospital having been temporarily blinded in a gas attack when he heard that Germany had capitulated. He was shattered by the news and was determined to continue the struggle by other means. With no prospects in civilian life, he applied in April 1919 for a position as an informer on political movements in Munich after the brutal crushing of a somewhat quixotic Munich Soviet Republic which was made up of sundry socialists, anarchists and communists. After attending a course of political instruction he was made a liaison officer between the Army and a recently formed Propaganda Unit. He was an instant success. His superiors commented that he was a 'born orator' who was fired with an admirable 'fanaticism' and always held his audience's attention. In a letter to his commanding officer he wrote that the first priority should be the application of 'rational anti-Semitism' that would lead to the 'removal of the Jews'. He was to hold this view until the bitter end in his bunker in Berlin.

Munich was a hotbed of small extremist groups in the immediate post-war years. One of these was the German Workers' Party (DAP) which Hitler visited in the course of his duties. Its fervent nationalism and virulent anti-Semitism were very much to his taste and he enrolled in the party as its 55th member in September 1919. On leaving the Army in May he devoted all his energies to the party, soon gaining a reputation as an electrifying beer-hall agitator. In society he was awkward and gauche, but in front of a crowd his demagogic skills were unsurpassed. In 1921 he took over the party which had been reorganized and renamed the National Socialist German Workers' Party (*Nationalsozialistische Deutsche Arbeiterpartei*, or NSDAP).

Hitler reinforced his position as leader (*Führer*) of the party by appointing his cronies to the managing committee, many of whom were recruited from the Thule Society, a grotesquely *völkisch* organization that was both wealthy and well-connected. These included Dietrich Eckart, an anti-Semitic scribbler who had a powerful influence in further inflaming Hitler's hatred of the Jews, which one clear-sighted observer had already described as 'pathological'. Alfred Rosenberg, a Baltic German whose racist *magnum opus* 'The Myth of the Twentieth Century' was so tedious that even Hitler found it unreadable, became the party's leading ideologue. Gottfried Feder was the party's economics expert with his diatribes against 'interest slavery' and 'Jewish capitalism'. Hans Frank, an unstable law student destined for high office and the hangman's noose, as well as Rudolph Hess, another rootless student soon to become Hitler's deputy, had both been in the Thule Society before joining the DAP.

Also among Hitler's closest associates in these early days were Max Amman, who ran the party's publishing house, Hermann Esser, who specialized in writing scurrilous accusations against prominent Jews for the party newspaper, the *Völkischer Beobachter*, and Julius Streicher, whose overbearing manner and sadistic Jew-baiting some more sensitive party members found crude and excessive. Ernst Röhm, a professional soldier and notorious homosexual, had close connections with the *Reichswehr* and procured arms for the party's paramilitary wing, the SA (*Sturmabteilung*), which in 1923 was commanded by Hermann Göring, a highly decorated veteran of the 'Richthofen Circus'. They were an unsavoury collection of youthful misfits, most of whom were about ten years younger than their 32-year-old leader.

From the outset Hitler was a demagogue rather than an organizer. Initially he had been reluctant to take on the chairmanship of the party in 1921. He was in no sense an original thinker and his much vaunted 'world view' (*Weltanschauung*) was little more than a garbage-pile of bitter resentments, mindless bigotry and malevolent prejudice, but it was made up of widely held views. By articulating the anxieties, hopes and fears of so many contemporaries, he met with an immediate response first in Bavaria and, within a remarkably short space of time, throughout Germany.

Hitler possessed the autodidact's absolute certainty that he was in the possession of the ideological key to an understanding of all the major questions of the day and the fanatical self-confidence that enabled him to convince others that this was indeed the case. He brooked no discussion among party members of the details of this devil's brew. The party was organized along military lines to obey the leadership and unquestioningly to disseminate its propaganda.

There were two principal components in Hitler's *Weltanschauung*: racial anti-Semitism and the need for 'living space' (*Lebensraum*). He believed that human history could be reduced to the struggle between races, or as he often phrased it 'peoples' (*Völker*). For a race, or *Volk*, to be strong it had to be pure. All harmful genetic material had to be destroyed, all alien elements eradicated. The aim of domestic politics, Hitler never tired of repeating, was the improvement of the 'racial value' of the *Volk* so as to give it the strength to carve out the *Lebensraum* essential for its survival. Politics was thus the eternal struggle of peoples and races for self-preservation. Samuel Beckett pointed out the absurdity of this vision when he said that the pure Aryan German should be: 'Blond like Hitler, thin like Göring, handsome like Goebbels, virile like Röhm – and called Rosenberg.'

Jews played an essential role within this primitive and atavistic imperialist and social-Darwinist vision. The Jews were stateless; unlike the Germans they had no imperative drive for *Lebensraum*. They were an alien and parasitic people that ate away like a cancer at the vital organs of the German *Volk*. Jews stood for everything that Hitler detested: democracy, internationalism, pacifism, communism, and all the unacceptable aspects of capitalism. Jews were filthy rich plutocrats and revoltingly poor beggars. They were capitalists and they were communists. They flaunted their wealth and their power, or they hid from view and plotted in secret. They murdered Jesus and they enfeebled the Aryan race with their compassionate morality that they passed on to Christianity. The Jew was thus symbolic of everything that was wrong with the modern world; all that stood in the way of the German people in their sacred struggle to achieve their rightful place as the master race. Julius Streicher claimed that since Jesus threw the moneylenders out of the temple he could not possibly have been a Jew, and should be included in the ranks of stalwart Aryan anti-Semites. Hitler shared this heterodox view and described Jesus as a 'great Aryan *Führer*' and prominent anti-Semite.

Hitler the myth-making artist also harboured aesthetic objections to the Jews. In *Mein Kampf* he claimed that it was the disgusting sight of an eastern Jew in a kaftan and with ringlets in Vienna that first turned him into a passionate anti-Semite. Henceforth he was determined to drive all these 'bow-legged, repulsive Jewish bastards' out of his Aryan Eden. He also shared Julius Streicher's sadistic, crude and sexually obsessed anti-Semitism.

Hitler's National Socialism was typical of fascist movements in the inter-war years in that it had a largely negative ideology. It was anti-democratic, anti-parliamentary, anti-liberal, anti-Marxist, anti-capitalist and anti-conservative. It proclaimed a racial nationalism and the 'socialism' of the racial community (*Volksgemeinschaft*), but these were half-baked expressions of what Hitler's entertaining and talented friend in the early Munich years, Ernst 'Putzi' Hanfstaengl, called his 'gnostic yearnings'. National Socialism, like Italian Fascism, never developed a coherent ideology analogous to Marxism-Leninism. What passed for ideology was little more than a ragbag of widely felt prejudices, rancour and spite that was full of staggering contradictions, boorish clichés, and empty-headed bigotry. In short it was a set of mutually reinforcing prejudices, but for all its intellectual poverty National Socialism offered an idealistic vision of a new society that had a wide appeal. Calls for national rebirth, for a real and meaningful sense of community, for employment and prosperity for all, and for an end to party political bickering may have been hollow and imprecise but they met with enthusiastic resonance. As Hitler pointed out in *Mein Kampf*, it was not cognition that counted, but blind faith.

The movement was thus not held together by intellectual conviction but by blind obedience to the *Führer*. He adjudicated between the warring factions within the party and was the sole interpreter of the canonical texts. Hitler never allowed himself to be bound by a party programme and avoided appealing to any narrow sectional interests. Charismatic leadership and skilful propaganda created the impression of a dynamic, disciplined and united party while at the same time enabling Hitler to change course whenever necessary. This consummate opportunist could thus appear as a man of principle; and conversely his fanatical racism and his lust for conquest, which remained undiminished until the bitter end, was partially hidden by his lofty station as a *Führer* who stood far above the humdrum political strife of his satraps, all criticism silenced by his astonishing record of success.

Within eighteen months Hitler established himself as an outstanding propagandist and adroit tactician who attracted widespread attention in the beer-halls of Munich. In the summer of 1921 he managed to oust Anton Drexler as party leader. He had no carefully considered plan to seize power, but as a masterly opportunist he threatened to resign from the party if the proposed amalgamation with another extremist group went ahead. The party could not afford to lose their star performer and appointed him leader with dictatorial powers. This incident is prototypical of Hitler the politician. It was a decision taken on the spur of the moment, all or nothing, the expression of his determination to let no one stand in his way and to impose his will on others.

The NSDAP gained national attention when Hitler attended the 'German Day' in Coburg in September 1922 accompanied by 800 SA men in their brown uniforms. They immediately became involved in a punch-up with the Social Democrats and thus won the reputation of being the most determined opponents of the Weimar Republic. Hitler launched a series of blistering attacks on the Republic and by 1923 referred to the fathers of the new state as the 'November criminals' who had betrayed the nation in November 1918 by signing an armistice even though the German Army claimed that it was undefeated.

Hitler the virtuoso demagogue attracted a considerable following during the crisis year of 1923. Membership rose from 15,000 to 55,000, but the party was still confined to Bavaria. He also began to win the support of wealthy benefactors, among them the anti-Semitic publisher Hugo Bruckmann, Carl Bechstein the piano manufacturer, and the steel magnate Fritz Thyssen. Elsa Bruckmann, a Romanian princess, and Helene Bechstein took a motherly interest in Hitler and were the first of the 'Hitler *Muttis*'. Both presented him with whips, which he always carried with him in these early days. He cut a bizarre figure in the fashionable salons of Munich as pistol-touting gangster, whip in hand, socially inept and patronized as an eccentric oddity by the city's élite.

Most of the members of the party came from the *petite bourgeoisie*, had been ruined by hyperinflation and faced an uncertain and threatening future. Contrary to Marxist myth the party appealed greatly to the working class and about one-third of the party members at this time came from a solidly proletarian background. As the myriad paramilitary organizations that plagued the Republic were gradually dissolved, many of their erstwhile members gravitated towards the SA. Hitler's denunciation of Versailles, the 'November criminals' and the 'system', and his call for a 'national revival', met with an eager response. He possessed the certainty of a sleepwalker that he was in the right, and the total conviction with which he expressed his views convinced others that what he said was indeed true. As Nietzsche pointed out in *Human, All Too Human*, men believe in the truth of all that is seen to be strongly believed. Hjalmar Schacht, the president of the Reichsbank and Hitler's first minister of economics, said of him: 'The thing that most impressed me about this man was his absolute conviction of the rightness of his outlook and his determination to translate this outlook into practical action.' Hitler soon discovered that the endless repetition of simplistic solutions to complex problems was the secret to success.

The SA expanded rapidly from being a group of beer-hall bouncers to a sizeable paramilitary organization with close links to the German Army (*Reichswehr*) in Bavaria, and it was largely independent from the party. The SA became even more autonomous when Ernst Röhm formed the Working Association of Patriotic Military Groups in January 1923. By the end of 1931 it had 260,000 members. Sharp differences between the party and its paramilitary wing on both strategy and tactics were only settled in the bloodbath of the 'Röhm putsch' of 1934.

1923: THE BEER-HALL PUTSCH

The early NSDAP was determined to overthrow the Weimar Republic and establish a fascist dictatorship on the Italian model. Hermann Esser proclaimed Hitler to be the 'German Mussolini' and the crisis year of 1923 raised hopes that Hitler could march on Berlin just as Mussolini had led the 'March on Rome' in October of the previous year.

The French occupation of the Ruhr in January 1923, when Germany had fallen badly behind in the payment of reparations, was seen by most Germans as an invasion and the nation was seized with patriotic fervour. The occupation was met with passive resistance, which in turn triggered off a fresh round of inflation, which soon got completely out of control to the point that money was not even worth the paper on which it was printed. By the summer a 10-pfennig telephone call cost 100 thousand million marks and an 84-pfennig loaf of white bread 840 thousand million. The Communist Party (KPD) was invited to join coalition governments in Saxony and Thuringia and plotted an uprising. A state of emergency was declared and the *Reichswehr* was sent in to root out the Communists. In Bavaria the former prime minister Gustav von Kahr seized power illegally, with the full support of the Bavarian units of the *Reichswehr* under General Otto Hermann von Lossow and of the chief of police Hans von Seisser.

Bavaria was thus in open defiance of the Republic and yet the *Reichswehr* refused to intervene as it had done against the Communists in Saxony and Thuringia. Enemies of the Weimar Republic now looked to Bavaria for deliverance. Hitler was in an awkward situation. He had been snubbed by the Kahr-Lossow-Seisser triumvirate which was now firmly in the saddle. History appeared to be in the making without his participation, and he felt increasingly isolated and deeply frustrated.

Without the support of the *Reichswehr* a nationwide putsch was bound to fail, and even if it were successful it would almost certainly result in French intervention. Nevertheless, Hitler was determined to stage a dramatic propaganda action that would put him in the spotlight and hopefully trigger off the 'German revolution' of which he had been dreaming for the last three years.

On 8 September Kahr invited all the various nationalist groups, with the exception of the NSDAP, to a rally in one of Munich's largest beer-halls, the Bürgerbräukeller. The meeting was well under way when it was rudely interrupted by Hitler and a small group of his followers that included Göring and Hess. In a state of great agitation, and firing his Browning at the ceiling, he announced that the 'national revolution' had broken out and that he was at the head of a new federal government. In a melodramatic scene, which he was frequently to repeat, he announced that should he fail he would commit suicide. He further warned that resistance was futile since the building was surrounded with machine guns.

Kahr and his conservative supporters protested vigorously and at first refused to give way to Hitler, but when Ludendorff arrived in the full-dress uniform of an imperial German general and gave Hitler his unconditional support they finally capitulated. After the announcement that a new federal government had been formed which included Ludendorff, Lossow and Seisser, with Kahr as plenipotentiary in Bavaria, the somewhat shaken

Kahr-Lossow-Seisser triumvirate was allowed to go home. They promptly ordered placards to be printed which announced that they had been forced at gunpoint to agree to the formation of this new government.

By the next day it was fairly obvious that this comic opera coup had failed, but Hitler ordered a march by the SA through the streets of Munich in a desperate bid to regain the initiative. The Bavarian police stopped the march just short of the Feldherrenhalle. Fire was exchanged, leaving fourteen Nazis and two policemen dead. The blood-soaked swastika flag became the party's holy relic, known as the 'Blood Flag', and 9 November was commemorated annually as 'Heroes Day'.

Hitler was arrested, and was tried on 1 April 1924. The proceedings were a mockery of justice, as was typical of many similar trials of right-wing extremists during the Weimar Republic. The court had kind words to say about Hitler's patriotism, idealism and courage and he was given the ridiculously light sentence of five years' imprisonment in a minimum-security facility in Landsberg with time off for good behaviour. Hitler spent of total of thirteen months in Landsberg, where he lived in modest comfort with plenty of free time to write *Mein Kampf*. The NSDAP was banned.

1924-1930: REBUILDING THE PARTY

The miserable failure of the attempted putsch convinced Hitler that he should win power by legal means, using the ballot box rather than the machine gun. To this end the NSDAP, which he rebuilt in February 1925 at a meeting in the Bürgerbräukeller within two months of his release from prison, was to be organized nationwide. It was to be clearly differentiated from other *völkisch* groups and was to be absolutely subservient to Hitler's will.

Hitler suffered another severe setback in March 1925 when the Bavarian government forbade him to speak in public. Most of the other German states followed suit. The party now had fewer than 30,000 members and was made up of a number of smaller groupings headed by sundry cranks and crackbrains, all of whom had leadership aspirations. Hitler could no longer mobilize mass support with his matchless demagogy, and this highly fissiparous party could only be held together by strict organization. But Hitler had no taste or talent for organization and left this humdrum work to his underlings. Of these the most important was Gregor Strasser who headed the 'Leadership Group' in northern Germany along with the

'Working Group of North-west German District Leaders' (*Gauleiter*). Strasser and his colleagues in the north formed a left-wing splinter group that emphasized the 'socialism' in National Socialism. Their views were propagated by the *Nationalsozialistischen Briefe* edited by Joseph Goebbels, and *Der Nationalsozialist*, whose editor was Gregor Strasser's brother Otto.

For all this left-wing allure, Gregor Strasser was a pragmatist who had excellent relations with the magnates of the Rhine and Ruhr. His differences with Hitler were fundamentally tactical, although expressed in ideological terms, and few outdid him in the fervour of his racism and anti-Semitism. He believed that efficient administration was the key to success whereas Hitler relied on the power of personality, on highly emotional propaganda, on endless struggle and restless movement.

At a party meeting held in Bamberg in February 1926 Hitler defied Gregor Strasser, who had proposed a drastic revision of the hopelessly naïve party programme that Anton Drexler had published on 24 February 1920 with its 25 points, which was said to be immutable. Hitler wanted no wrangling over the finer points of ideology, since he saw himself as the sole arbiter in such matters. Strasser grumbled about Hitler's reactionary views, but was not the man to stand up and fight. He continued his work building up the party in northern Germany and did so to great effect. Goebbels, who loathed Gregor Strasser while being in broad agreement with his politics, was won over completely to Hitler's point of view and remained his ardent acolyte until they died together in the Berlin bunker.

Hitler also faced off with the SA in early 1925, but in this struggle he could at least rely on Gregor Strasser's support. Ernst Röhm wanted the SA to be an independent paramilitary force that worked closely with similar organizations. Hitler insisted that it should remain strictly within the bounds of legality and be unconditionally submissive to the political will of the party and ultimately to him as *Führer*. Hitler once again triumphed and Röhm left Germany in disgust, accepting a post as military advisor to the Bolivian government.

Gregor Strasser was an organizational genius who, in spite of his many outstanding differences with Hitler, worked tirelessly at building the party. It is largely due to him that Hitler had at his command a tightly organized political apparatus. Party headquarters were in Munich, and Germany was divided into 30 and later 36 districts (*Gaue*) each with a district leader (*Gauleiter*) many of whom were appointed by Gregor Strasser, but all of whom professed absolute loyalty to the *Führer*. Each district was divided into wards (*Ortsgruppen*) with a ward leader (*Ortsgruppenleiter*). The wards were subdivided into cells (*Zellen*) with a cell leader (*Zellenleiter*). The smallest organizational unit was the block (*Block*) with its *Blockleiter*, who kept a close watch on his neighbours. A host of other organizations were also formed, among them the National Socialist German Students Association (NSDStB) in 1926, the Association of National Socialist Lawyers in 1928, the National Socialist German Medical Association in the following year, and the National Socialist Factory Cell Organization (NSBO) in 1930. Special organizations were also formed to deal with such matters as foreign policy, legal questions and the press.

For all its divisions and factions the party was held together by its devotion to Hitler. Even Gregor Strasser was unquestioningly behind this cult of the personality, in spite of continuing tactical and ideological differences with Hitler. All 'party comrades' (PGs) now had to greet one another with '*Heil Hitler!*' and the party's youth organization was named the Hitler Youth (HJ). Goebbels became the high priest of the *Führer* cult and skillfully masked internal political conflicts with clouds of propagandistic incense.

Hitler was a perfect example of what Max Weber called 'charismatic leadership'. He did not inherit this position, nor did he achieve it by formal, legal or bureaucratic means. It was an entirely personal authority based on a widespread need among the masses to find a saviour, a hero and a message. For all his intellectual poverty he was somehow able to project an idealistic vision of new society that struck a chord with millions. The *terrible simplificateur* who came from nowhere appeared as a Parsifal or a Siegfried, a holy simpleton who would bring salvation from a deep-rooted ontological crisis by disregarding the complexities of modern society and by concentrating on the essentials: the nation, the race, the dangers posed by Jews and Bolshevism and the need for *Lebensraum*. This certainly did not have universal appeal. In 1928 Germany's finest newspaper, the *Frankfurter Zeitung*, described Hitler as a man possessed by a demon, driven by a manic idea of atavistic origin, a dangerous fool from the time of the barbarian invasions.

A charismatic *Führer* could not allow himself to be bound by any organization, and Hitler resisted all Strasser's attempts to establish an ordered bureaucratic chain of command within the party. He surrounded himself with a group of trusted vassals who owed him their total allegiance and who acted as intermediaries between the *Führer* and the party. Within the party there was an endless struggle for power between personalities and groups and only the fittest survived. Hitler encouraged this chaotic state of affairs because it left him isolated above the petty squabbles of his underlings, and this curious political form of natural selection was very much to his taste. On the other hand, without Strasser's organizational genius the NSDAP would never have become a mass party, and Hitler would not have been appointed chancellor. When Strasser was pushed aside in 1932 the party once again was rent with factional squabbles and once Hitler was in power it was allowed to atrophy.

The first major test for the new party came with the presidential elections in March 1925 occasioned by Friedrich Ebert's sudden death. In the first round of the elections the NSDAP supported General Ludendorff, who only managed to garner 285,000 votes. This was a disappointing result, but it had the great advantage for Hitler that it removed his only serious contender on the extremist right. The NSDAP gained 2.6 per cent of the vote in the Reichstag elections in 1928, which gave them twelve seats. By the end of 1929 they had 48 delegates elected to the various provincial parliaments.

1930-1933: THE PATH TO VICTORY

The NSDAP's startling breakthrough in the Reichstag elections of 1930 was a direct result of the economic and political crisis that brought the Weimar Republic to its knees. The devastating effects of the depression, which had already begun to be felt as early as the winter of 1928, was combined with a political crisis that resulted in the suspension of normal parliamentary procedure and rule by presidential decree. The Reichstag met for a total of thirteen days throughout 1932. The democratic system no longer worked, and the bureaucratic apparatus was unable to bring any relief. Millions of Germans were without work and abandoned all hope for the future. The National Socialists played on the fears, anxieties and exasperation of the masses. They laid the blame for the present wretched state of affairs on Versailles, the 'November Criminals', parliamentary democracy, Communists and Jews. They promised strong leadership and radical measures that would lead Germany forward into a glorious future. The German people were not bamboozled, bewitched or baffled by Hitler. He provided the vision, the leadership, the determination and the sense of community for which they yearned.

The NSDAP was without question Hitler's party, but he would never have met with such success were it not for the devoted support of his gifted subordinates. Goebbels devoted his prodigious talents as a propagandist to the cult of the *Führer*. Gregor Strasser, for all his ideological differences with Hitler, was a devotee who gave the party an organizational structure that reinforced the *Führer's* position, disciplined the membership, and made possible the mass demonstrations, marches and rallies that helped reinforce the impression that National Socialism was a vibrant, vigorous and dynamic movement in sharp contrast to the bankrupt traditional parties of the Weimar Republic.

The majority of Germans were still immune to the siren calls of National Socialism, at least in the years before 1933. Its anti-clericalism, its pagan rituals and Hitler's messianic pretensions appalled most Catholics. The majority of the working class remained faithful to the Social Democrats and the Communists, although an increasing number of workers from smaller firms and independent craftsmen who had not previously been politically active flocked to the party from 1930 onwards. Many conservatives had serious reservations about Hitler. They dismissed him as a vulgar upstart, were appalled by his absurd ideas about the economy and his approval of the lawless violence of the SA. On the other hand, many members of the upper class yearned for an authoritarian solution to Germany's problems and were reassured by Hitler's protestations that his more radical ideas were simply designed to catch votes and should not be taken seriously.

Paradoxically, the party which was founded in Catholic Bavaria and still had its headquarters in Munich was most successful in the Protestant north and east, especially in rural areas. Those who were worst hurt by the depression, who saw no hope for the future, who despised the parliamentary system that had so miserably failed, and who found socialism repugnant were easily won over. These included a large number of minor civil servants, small businessmen, farmers and white-collar workers. In the years from 1930 to 1932, 54.9 per cent of the members of the party belonged to this *petite bourgeoisie*. In contrast, 35.9 per cent came from the lower orders, 9.2 per cent from the upper class.

Above all the party was, like the Communist Party (KPD), remarkably youthful. It was also largely male. It was widely believed that Hitler's success was based on the adulation of the opposite sex. In fact only 7.8 per cent of those joining the party between 1925 and 1932 were women. By 1930 70 per cent of party members were under the age of 40 and 37 per cent under the age of 30. Hitler was 41, Göring 37, Goebbels 33 and Himmler 30.

With its membership drawn from all walks of life, the NSDAP could present itself as a genuine people's party, the party for the whole German *Volk*. Its youthfulness made it appear as the vigorous and idealistic harbinger of a bright future. Voters also came from all classes. The hard core of support came from the urban lower-middle class and the peasantry. By 1930 white collar workers and pensioners began to vote for the NSDAP in large numbers, and many members of the upper class overcame their previous reservations and lent the party their support. They made fewer inroads in the big cities where Communists and Social Democrats maintained their share of the vote. Similarly in Catholic areas voters remained faithful to the Catholic Centre Party.

A vast and complex organization such as the NSDAP needed a great deal of money. Until the party made its great breakthrough in 1930 it was financed largely by members' dues, entrance fees for the major party events, and collections at rallies. Donations also came from wealthy sympathizers and small businessmen. In the early years very little money came from big business interests. Fritz Thyssen and Paul Silverberg were exceptions, and most industrialists supported the idea of an authoritarian government headed by Franz von Papen or Kurt von Schleicher that would bypass parliament and rule by presidential decree. Inasmuch as these industrialists helped to destroy parliamentary democracy, they helped to prepare the way for Adolf Hitler, and once he was in power he could count on their full support.

The big breakthrough came in 1929, when Hitler decided to join the conservative nationalists (DNVP) and right-wing veterans' organization *Stahlhelm* (Steel Helmet) in the referendum campaign against the Young Plan for a final settlement of Germany's reparations. For many National Socialists, particularly on the left of the party, this was a betrayal of party principles. The leadership was now hobnobbing with men whom they had previously denounced as 'plutocrats' and 'reactionaries', and the anti-capitalist party programme had to be abandoned along with all hopes of weaning the working class away from the Marxist parties. But the positive results of this dramatic change of course were impressive. Although only 14 per cent voted in favour in the referendum, the Nazis had become respectable. Those who had had serious reservations about the party's radicalism now joined in droves. 19,000 new members were registered in November alone and within a few weeks the party had 200,000 members.

The NSDAP tripled its vote in regional elections in Thuringia where Wilhelm Frick, one of the more repulsive members of Hitler's unsavoury inner circle, was appointed minister of the interior. He promptly set about closing down Germany's most exciting art school, the Bauhaus, which he deemed to be a den of 'Jewish-Bolshevik' art. He also established a chair for Race Research at the University of Jena.

Federal elections were held in September 1930 when the Chancellor, Heinrich Brüning, failed to find a majority for his austerity measures and the Reichstag refused to grant him emergency powers under Article 48 of the constitution. The NSDAP conducted a brilliant campaign promising to end the endless squabbling of the discredited political parties, and painting a vivid picture of the classless, vigorous and united society of the 'racial community' (*Volksgemeinschaft*). Above all they promised dynamic leadership and in Adolf Hitler they had a spellbinding orator who travelled tirelessly the length and breadth of Germany addressing huge crowds of enthusiastic proselytes.

The result exceeded even Hitler's wildest expectations. Support for the Nazis increased almost ninefold. They now had 18.3 per cent of the popular vote, giving them 107 seats in place of twelve. At 82 per cent, voter participation was unusually high and many first-time voters gave their support to the NSDAP. The big losers were the *bourgeois* parties: the Conservatives (DNVP), the Democrats (DDP) and the People's Party (DVP). Here voters had clearly switched their allegiance to a party that was now deemed fit for polite society. The other big winners were the Communists with 13.1 per cent of the popular vote. This too worked in the Nazis' favour. The election results were a declaration of the bankruptcy of the parliamentary system. Politics had become polarized to the extent that many began to feel that they were faced with a choice between the Nazis and the Communists. For these there was no real choice at all.

The political landscape of Germany was permanently altered by these election results. Before September 1930 many looked back to the good old days of the monarchy as an alternative to parliamentary democracy. Now the alternative seemed to be to modify the constitution along authoritarian lines or an outright dictatorship. The parties on the right and the *Reichswehr* hoped that the National Socialists would agree to a coalition government in which they would be obliged to moderate their views. Others, like Otto Braun, the outstanding social democratic prime minister of Prussia, wondered how best to confront the Nazi threat. The Centre Party, which had been one of the great supporters of Weimar democracy, had moved drastically to the right under its new leader Ludwig Kaas, a priest who detested the Social Democrats and sought an accommodation with the conservatives. The Catholic bishops were still determined to keep their distance and published a number of denunciations of National Socialism. The Communists were indifferent. They saw the Nazis as just another capitalist party, indistinguishable from all the others, including the Social

Democrats. That left the Social Democrats as the only party determined to save democracy in Germany; but too many socialists were ideologically rigid and objected to the idea of co-operating with the *bourgeois* parties.

New supporters flocked to the National Socialists as the economic and political crisis deepened, but this placed Hitler in an increasingly awkward position. The expectations of the party faithful were running high, but it was difficult to see how he could meet them. He refused to enter into any coalition as a junior partner, and it seemed unlikely that he could achieve power by legal means. There were many within the ranks of the SA who felt that revolutionary violence was the only answer.

Initially Corporal Hitler had been uncertain whether to run against the field marshal in the presidential elections held in April 1932. He dithered for a month, driving his followers to despair, until he finally decided. First he had to become a German citizen. This was done by getting himself appointed counsellor (*Regierungsrat*) in the Surveyor's Office in Braunschweig. By thus becoming a civil servant, he automatically acquired citizenship. Once again he ran a tireless and brilliant campaign, dashing all over the country, using the aeroplane to great effect with the slogan 'Hitler over Germany'. Hitler won 36.8 per cent of the vote to Hindenburg's 53 per cent. It was a remarkable result, but to impatient Nazi radicals it seemed like a defeat.

In May 1932 Hindenburg appointed von Papen chancellor. With the NSDAP and the Communists holding the majority of seats in the Reichstag he had no alternative but to rule by emergency presidential decrees. His 'New Course' was a grotesquely reactionary programme based on the confused musings of the Austrian neo-romantic Othmar Spann, which promised to root out 'cultural Bolshevism', assert 'Christian principles' and replace parliamentary government with a society based on the estates. On 20 July he took the dramatic and unconstitutional step of suspending the government of Prussia led by the Social Democrat Otto Braun, a deter-mined opponent of the National Socialists, on the pretext that it could not guarantee law and order in the face of mounting political violence. Papen took over the office of Prussian prime minister and he appointed a commissar to act as minister of the interior. Germany's largest state was now ruled from Berlin, and Prussian officials with democratic sympathies were summarily dismissed and replaced by stalwart conservatives.

In June Papen also revoked the ban on the SA which Brüning and Groener had implemented in April. The result was a fresh round of violence that pushed Germany to the brink of civil war. It was in this tense atmosphere that Papen called for Reichstag elections in July. The NSDAP more than doubled its share of the vote to 37.3 per cent and obtained 230 seats making them the largest faction, well ahead of the next largest party, the SPD, with their 133 seats. But this was still not enough, and Goebbels noted in his diary that the party would never win a majority and would therefore have to find some other way to attain power. The party had either to abandon legality or settle for a power-sharing arrangement. Gregor Strasser warned that the party was running desperately short of funds and suggested that it should concentrate on coalition building.

On 13 August Hindenburg granted Hitler a brief interview in which he flatly refused to appoint him chancellor. Shortly afterwards Papen's government published a communiqué from Hindenburg in which the aged president stated that he owed it to 'God, my conscience and the fatherland' not to give the chancellorship to a man like Hitler who was bent on dictatorship.

Papen went ahead with his plans for the 'New State', but he had virtually no support. The SA became increasingly frustrated and violent. The unions planned a general strike in protest against the government's austerity measures. In a desperate attempt to gain parliamentary endorsement for his authoritarian schemes, Papen called another round of elections in November. This time the Nazis suffered a serious decline in support, their share in the popular vote dropping from 37.3 to 33.1 per cent. This was in part due to their endorsement of the Communist-led strike by the Berlin transport workers, thus clearly distancing themselves from the 'reactionaries' in the DNVP. The Communists increased their share from 14.3 to 16.9 per cent. The anti-democratic parties could thus still turn down any proposal put before the Reichstag and Papen could not possibly create his 'New State'.

General Kurt von Schleicher, a political intriguer who had the president's ear and who had been instrumental in securing Papen's appointment, now decided to drop his protégé and got himself appointed as chancellor at the beginning of December. He hoped to make a broad coalition, which would include the trades unions and the left-wing Nazis around Gregor Strasser, to whom he offered the post of vice-chancellor. His government would put Germany back to work with an ambitious programme of public spending and restore the welfare programmes that Papen had abolished.

Strasser was inclined to accept. Hitler began to panic, fearing that he would lose control of the party and he made yet another dramatic threat to commit suicide. The sense of resignation and helplessness that was widespread throughout German society was beginning to affect the party. There were ominous signs that the party was falling apart, but he quickly recovered his composure and, steeled by Goebbels and Göring, fought back. Gregor Strasser lost his nerve and threw in the towel, resigning from all his party offices. The trades unions did not trust Schleicher and refused to co-operate. The agrarians and most of the influential industrialists thought that Schleicher's programme smacked of socialism, and began to think of Hitler as a viable alternative. The chancellor thus had virtually no support and Papen saw his chance to get his revenge. Hitler was now a tragic accident about to happen.

Papen imagined that he could manipulate Hitler, whose position seemed far from secure. The Nazis had suffered a severe setback in the November elections and the party was further weakened by the Strasser affair and the growing impatience of the SA. Editorial writers proclaimed National Socialism to be a spent force and a number of leading Nazis gloomily admitted that they were probably right.

On 4 January Papen met Hitler at the home of a mutual acquaintance, the Cologne banker Baron Kurt von Schröder, and offered him the chancellorship in a joint cabinet. It seemed like a vain gesture. Papen had virtually no support, his career to date having been a series of remarkable disasters, and Hindenburg was known to dislike Hitler intensely. But there was mounting concern in conservative circles about Schleicher's socialistic experiments. Some leading generals, foremost among them Werner von Blomberg, were alarmed at Schleicher's suggestion that a military dictatorship might provide a temporary solution and were sympathetic to the idea of a Hitler/Papen government. Hitler after all promised rearmament, a larger army and a more forceful foreign policy. Other generals disliked the plebeian Nazis' radicalism and lawless violence, and were deeply suspicious of the SA. A scandal involving financial aid for agriculture in eastern Germany (*Osthilfe*) caused the agrarians to be more sympathetic to Hitler, and they had the president's ear. A Hitler/Papen government would have a majority in the Reichstag, it would no longer be necessary to rule by presidential decree, contemplate acting unconstitutionally or risk a civil war. Above all Hindenburg was fond of Papen, whom he called 'Fränzchen', and felt that Schleicher had done no better than his predecessor. On 28 January Hindenburg, having consulted Papen, refused to continue granting Schleicher emergency powers. He was determined to appoint a government which had a parliamentary majority and which would thus not need to use Article 48. A Hitler government was now a virtual certainty. After two days of frantic discussions, during which the president was convinced that Hitler's bid for a one-party dictatorship would fail for lack of parliamentary support, he was finally appointed chancellor on 30 January 1933.

two

THE CONSOLIDATION
OF POWER

31 January 1933–1 August 1934

JANUARY TO JULY 1933: HITLER AS CHANCELLOR

The conservative élite was delighted that there was only one other
National Socialist in Hitler's first cabinet: Wilhelm Frick, who was
appointed minister of the interior. The conservatives still controlled the
civil service, the army and the judiciary and enjoyed the support of the
agrarians and the industrialists. Hitler the drummer boy provided the mass
support that they had hitherto lacked. Papen spoke on their behalf when
he announced: 'He is now in our employ!' and added: 'In two months' time
we will have pushed Hitler so tightly into the corner that he will squeak!'
The Stahlhelm leader Theodor Duesterberg, who refused a position in
Hitler's cabinet, claimed that Hitler would soon be seen running in his
underpants through the chancellery garden to avoid arrest. It seemed to be
a perfect solution: Hitler's popularity, drive and dynamism were harnessed
by experienced and responsible conservatives.

   This was an astonishing misreading of the situation, as the DNVP leader
and minister of economics, Hugenberg, was soon to admit. The conservative élites completely overlooked the fact that behind a threadbare façade
the Weimar Republic was falling apart. Society was in the midst of a
profound crisis, and for all his moderate assurances in the last few days,
Hitler was a man with a fanatical determination to destroy the existing state
and establish an iron dictatorship. His clearly stated intention to call
elections as soon as possible should have been indication enough to his
conservative allies that he was out to destroy them, and that his assurances
to the DNVP had to be taken with a great deal of salt. The Nazis had mass

support and a superb propaganda machine, and the SA was more than happy to resort to violence whenever necessary. Precious little stood in their way.

The two great working-class parties, the Social Democrats (SPD) and the Communists (KPD), were caught completely by surprise on 30 January. Both parties managed to convince themselves the Hitler was little more than a marionette with sinister capitalists pulling the strings and that he would soon outdo his usefulness. The Communists still clung to their absurd theory of 'social fascism' whereby the main enemy of the proletariat was not the Nazis but the Social Democrats. The Social Democrats had still not recovered from the shock of Papen's coup against their stronghold in Prussia on 20 July. A general strike was unthinkable at the height of the depression with millions unemployed. Such was the animosity between the SPD and KPD that even if they had opened their eyes to the mortal danger that threatened them, they would not have been able to stand together in an anti-Fascist front. The Social Democrats were overcome with a sense of helpless resignation. The Communists dismissed the Nazis as just another *bourgeois* party.

At the time of the Nazi seizure of power there were some 850,000 party members. They mounted a series of torchlight processions and heralded the 'national revolution'. Sceptical intellectuals like Count Harry Kessler dismissed such demonstrations as a mere carnival. Others waited anxiously upon events. Most Germans were indifferent, and there was no rush to join the party. Only after the March elections was there a scramble to jump on the bandwagon. These opportunists, contemptuously known as the 'March Fallen' (*Märzgefallenen*) by the old guard, were so numerous that by January 1934 the membership had almost trebled.

Hitler's first announcement of his long-term goals was made behind closed doors to a group of leading generals on 3 February. He certainly did not mince his words. He promised strict authoritarian rule that would rid Germany of the 'cancer' of democracy, 'exterminate' Marxism and pacifism and make Germany once again ready for war (*Wiederwehrhaftmachung*) by rearmament and the introduction of universal military service. In an ominous footnote, which most of his audience seems to have overheard, he spoke of 'radically Germanizing' the east in order to carve out 'living space' (*Lebensraum*). The generals with their traditional anti-Semitism, their loathing for 'Jewish Bolshevism', their determination to rearm and to revise the Versailles settlement were encouraged by these remarks. For all their snobbish disdain towards some of the more vulgar aspects of National

Socialism, they were in broad agreement with Hitler's programme, and most of them remained so until the bitter end.

On 1 February Hindenburg agreed to dissolve the Reichstag and elections were called for 5 March. In the meantime Hitler could make use of the emergency presidential powers as provided in Article 48 of the Weimar constitution. He could count on wide support and he complacently remarked at the cabinet meeting on 1 February that this was to be the last Reichstag election, and there would be no return to the parliamentary system.

On 4 February Hitler used the Communist appeal for a general strike as an excuse to push through an emergency decree 'for the protection of the German people'. It permitted severe restrictions on the freedom of the press and of assembly should there be 'an immediate danger to public safety', or in instances where 'the organs, organizations and offices of the state and its employees were insulted or mocked'. This gave Hitler and his minions discretion to silence the opposition parties during the election campaign. Appeals against the flagrant misuse of this decree could be made to the High Court (*Reichsgericht*), but by the time they could be lodged the election was long since over.

Hermann Göring used the decree to the utmost in Prussia where he had been appointed minister of the interior in the commissarial government. Otto Braun's government had been reinstated when the State Court (*Staatsgerichtshof*) ruled that Papen's coup in July 1932 was unconstitutional, so that there were now two governments in Prussia. Hitler then issued another presidential decree 'for the restoration of orderly government in Prussia' and on 6 February the Prussian parliament (*Landtag*) was once again dissolved.

Although Göring was formally subordinate to Papen as Reich Commissar for Prussia, he promptly weeded out the few remaining democrats in the upper echelons of the Prussian civil service, police force and judiciary. The Prussian secret police was reorganized into a separate Secret Police Office (*Geheimes Staatspolizeiamt – Gestapa*). The police were ordered to co-operate fully with the SA, the SS and the *Stahlhelm* in an all-out campaign against the Communists. Meetings of all the democratic parties were systematically broken up, politicians were brutally beaten within an inch of their lives, and the opposition press silenced. On 17 February Göring published a decree in which he ordered the police to shoot to kill if necessary, and guaranteed that he would protect any officer who found it necessary to use his gun.

The SA was given *carte blanche* to disrupt the meetings of republican parties, to beat up politicians, threaten officials, and make arbitrary arrests. Their hapless victims were flung into hastily improvised concentration camps. Thus a former minister, Adam Stegerwald of the Centre Party, was brutally assaulted during a rally in Krefeld. The Social Democratic police president of Berlin, Albert Grzesinski, was made to fear for his life and obliged to resign. The offices of a number of republican newspapers were torched. In all there were 69 deaths and hundreds were seriously wounded during the five weeks of the election campaign. The SA arrested some 100,000 people in the early months of 1933, and murdered about 600. There was widespread revulsion against such barbarity. Ludendorff, Hitler's brother-in-arms in 1923, wrote to his old superior Hindenburg complaining bitterly about such 'unbelievable events' and claiming that this was 'the blackest time in German history'.

Hitler travelled tirelessly the length and breadth of Germany preaching his simple message of national redemption to vast and enthusiastic crowds. He denounced the 'November criminals' who were responsible for the last fourteen years of economic misery, political bickering and national humiliation. He promised to unite the nation into a strong-willed 'racial community' (*Volksgemeinschaft*) that would transcend all divisions of class and station. The economy would be revitalized in two successive four-year plans. 'National rebirth' would result from reasserting family values and Christian morality. He made no concrete proposals, but he spoke with such utter conviction and passion that the crowds believed that he could be trusted. In this highly charged emotional atmosphere what mattered was not a carefully crafted programme but a spontaneous and passionate reaction. The opposition forces were so hopelessly divided, demoralized and cowed that they could offer little resistance.

On 20 February Hitler addressed a group of leading industrialists and told them that this would be positively the last election and that he intended to create a strong and independent state, regardless of the outcome of the election. First he had to gain absolute power, and then he would destroy his opponents. The industrialists were delighted, and promptly got out their chequebooks and relieved the party of all financial worries.

At nine o'clock in the evening of 27 February smoke was seen billowing through the roof of the Reichstag. Shortly afterwards a dim-witted Dutch anarchist, Marinus van der Lubbe, was arrested in the Bismarck Room and promptly admitted that he had set the building on fire. The National

Socialists convinced themselves that this was part of a Communist plot. Their opponents claimed that the Nazis had organized the fire in order to find an excuse to bring in further emergency legislation. The Communists soon published a 'Brown Book' which purported to show Nazi complicity in the fire and which proved to be a highly effective piece of anti-fascist propaganda.

The Nazi claim that van der Lubbe was under orders from the Communists was soon shown to be utterly false. Communists later admitted that the 'Brown Book' was a fabrication. In 1962 Fritz Tobias published a detailed study of the Reichstag fire and came to the conclusion that van der Lubbe acted alone. Most historians now accept this version, although some respected scholars still believe that the Nazis were implicated.

Regardless of who was ultimately responsible for the fire, the Nazis acted promptly. When Hitler was told of the fire he wound himself up into a passion and said that all Communist functionaries should be shot and Reichstag deputies hanged. The Prussian ministry of the interior promptly set about drafting an emergency decree. On the following day the 'decree for the protection of the People and the State' was promulgated. All the fundamental rights guaranteed in the constitution were suspended. The death penalty was extended to include a number of crimes including treason and arson. Summary arrests could be made and the Nazis' opponents were placed in 'protective custody' in concentration camps. In an important step towards dismantling the Republic's federal structure, Wilhelm Frick as minister of the interior could disregard the sovereignty of the states if he deemed that law and order were in jeopardy. This decree, which claimed to be solely directed against the Communists, was the fundamental law on which the Nazi dictatorship was based. It remained in force even though van der Lubbe's trial in September clearly showed that there was no evidence that the Communists were involved. The accused was executed even though arson was not a capital offence at the time he committed the crime. There was a wave of arrests throughout Germany. 100,000 people, mostly Communists, were arrested in Prussia, among them the prominent left-wing writers Egon Erwin Kisch, Erich Mühsam, Carl von Ossietsky and Ludwig Renn.

In spite of all the intimidation, mass arrests and harassment of the opposition parties, the results of the elections were most disappointing for the National Socialists. They only managed to obtain 43.9 per cent of the popular vote, 6.6 percentage points more than their best showing in the July elections of 1932. Their largest gains were in Bavaria and Württemberg, where they had previously had little support. Since the conservatives got a meagre 8 per cent, the coalition parties had a very narrow majority in the Reichstag. Voters remained faithful to the Social Democrats and the Centre Party, and the Communists did surprisingly well under the circumstances with 12.3 per cent. The parties in the middle of the political spectrum were virtually eliminated. The astonishingly high voter participation of 88.8 per cent showed how important these elections were to the average German.

The ballots were hardly counted when the National Socialists set about the demolition of the Republic's federal structure. A two-pronged attack on local government was launched. SA thugs and party activists stormed town halls and local government offices, hoisted the swastika flag and chased terrified officials away. The authorities in Berlin used such lawlessness as an excuse to overthrow provincial governments by using the powers vested in them in Article 2 of the Reichstag Fire Decree. Commissars, often the local *Gauleiter*, were appointed in each of the states and prominent Nazis replaced the police chiefs.

In some areas the Nazis met with considerable resistance. The Bavarian prime minister Heinrich Held adamantly refused to give way to threats from the SA, but the local army units gave him no support when ordered from Berlin to stay out of domestic politics. Hitler's wooing of the Reichswehr on 3 February thus paid a handsome dividend. Held was now without any support and Frick appointed the stalwart Nazi Lieutenant-General Franz Ritter von Epp as commissar for Bavaria. The commissar's protégé Heinrich Himmler, head of the still minute SS, was made chief of police in Munich and then took over the Bavarian secret police. Ably assisted by his ruthless and brilliant underling Reinhard Heydrich, this was the beginning of a remarkable career in law enforcement.

On 21 March, the first day of spring, the regime held an impressive ceremony in Potsdam organized by Joseph Goebbels, who had recently been appointed minister of propaganda. The occasion was designed not only to mark the opening of the new parliament, but also as a symbolic gesture of reconciliation between the old and the new Germany. Representatives of all walks of life were present. Only the Communists and the Social Democrats were not invited because, as Frick remarked with obvious relish, they had a lot of important work to do in the concentration camps.

The 'Potsdam Day' began with a service in the garrison church after which Hitler was presented to Hindenburg. The humble other-ranker bowed before the field marshal. Hindenburg then saluted the empty chair where the Kaiser used to sit and behind which stood the crown prince. Hitler gave an anodyne speech in which he spoke of the union of past greatness with youthful vigour. National Socialism was thus presented as the apotheosis of German history in the long and glorious tradition of Luther, Frederick the Great, Bismarck and Hindenburg. Goebbels was well satisfied with the day's work, which he cynically described in his diary as a 'jolly farce'.

The atmosphere was menacing when the Reichstag met three days later in the Kroll Opera House in Berlin. The SA surrounded it, Hitler appeared in party uniform, all of the 81 Communist deputies were forbidden to attend and 26 Social Democrats had been arrested. There was only one item of business on the agenda: a constitutional amendment that would put an end to the last vestiges of parliamentary rule and known as the 'Enabling Act'.

Since the bill needed a two-thirds majority, all depended on the attitude of the Centre Party. The leadership under Monsignor Ludwig Kaas favoured an authoritarian solution to the present crisis, and feared that opposition would result in further restrictions of the freedom of the Catholic Church. Others managed to convince themselves that the bill was aimed solely against the Communists and comforted themselves with the thought that it was only to last for four years. The former chancellor Heinrich Brüning had serious reservations. After lengthy discussions the party agreed to vote for the proposal. Otto Wels from the Social Democratic party was the only member who had the courage to speak out against the bill. His measured but passionate plea for democracy, the rule of law and the fundamental principles of his party incited Hitler's fury, but had no influence on the outcome. There were 444 votes in favour and only 94 against. Even though the bill had been pushed through in a blatantly unconstitutional manner it was formally renewed twice, and thus provided the pseudo-legal basis for twelve years of dictatorship.

On 31 March the government used its new powers to promulgate the Provisional Law for the Co-ordination (*Gleichschaltung*) of the States (*Länder*) with the Reich. This gave state governments the right to pass legis-lation without consulting regional parliaments. State governors (*Reichsstatthälter*), who acted on instructions from Berlin, were appointed under the terms of a second bill of 7 April. Hitler appointed himself *Reichsstatthalter* of Prussia, but delegated his authority to Göring. Thus ended the long tradition of German federalism.

The new system was greatly confused by the fact that many of the *Reichsstatthälter* were also *Gauleiter*, but the state and party district boundaries did not correspond. It was typical of the Third Reich that this resulted in a confusion of state and party functions, as well as power struggles where state and district boundaries overlapped. The situation was further muddled when Armaments Commissars were appointed in areas which corresponded to neither the states nor the party districts. Furthermore the *Gauleiter* and state governors established themselves as little Hitlers in their satrapies, paying little attention to instructions passed down from Berlin, and considering themselves beholden to the *Führer* alone.

For all the talk of the unity of the National Socialist state, there was thus from the very beginning a hopeless confusion of state and party, federal and state competence, the government and special plenipotentiaries. Hitler was in many ways a 'hands-off' tyrant. He preferred to let his myrmidons struggle among themselves and let the strongest and fittest emerge triumphant. This corresponded to his view of life as an endless struggle and it ensured that the Nazi movement never lost its activist dynamic by becoming bureaucratized. The end result was that the leading figures in the Third Reich were almost without exception a repulsive collection of brutish gangsters, corrupt place-seekers and ruthless careerists. The advantage of this administrative *Blitzkrieg* was that it was possible to cut through red tape and avoid futile paper shuffling, but far too much time and energy was lost on interdepartmental rivalries and the struggle for power.

In June 1934 a senior civil servant wrote to Frick: 'Legally the state governors are subordinate to you as minister of the interior. Adolf Hitler is the state governor of Prussia. He has delegated his authority to Göring. You are also Prussian minister of the interior. As Reich minister of the interior, Adolf Hitler and the Prussian prime minister are legally subordinate to you. Since you are the same person as the Prussian prime minister you are subordinate to the Prussian prime minister and to yourself as Reich minister of the interior. I am not a legal scholar, but I am sure that such a situation has never happened before.'

The regime now set about the systematic destruction of the political parties that no longer had any role to play after the passing of the Enabling Act. On 1 May Goebbels staged a 'Day of National Labour'. On the following day the trades unions were banned. Units of the SA and SS stormed union offices and union leaders were arrested. Although most leading Communists had been imprisoned or had fled the country after the Reichstag fire, the party had not been forbidden, so as to ensure that the working-class vote would be split in the March election. The party was not formally banned until the end of March. Moscow appeared curiously indifferent to the destruction of the party and the martyrdom of its members.

The Social Democratic paramilitary organization *Reichsbanner*, which had been involved in a series of street battles with the SA, was banned state by state. The party had been harassed since the Reichstag fire decree, its party offices raided, its newspapers banned. The membership was demoralized and rapidly dwindled. Many of the leadership moved to Prague whence they called for an all out struggle against Hitler's regime. The Nazis used this as an excuse to ban the party on 22 June and ordered the arrest of all those party leaders who were still in Germany.

The smaller democratic parties self-destructed so that now only the Centre Party, its Bavarian branch party (BVP) and the conservatives (DNVP) remained. Members were leaving these parties in droves, many of them joining the National Socialists. On 28 March the Catholic bishops, fearing that the state might interfere with the church, made a solemn pledge of allegiance to the Nazi State. Monsignor Kaas was in Rome discussing the details of a concordat with Papen and Vatican officials, so the party was left leaderless. Brüning took over command on 6 May, but the party had no fight left in it. Under the terms of the Concordat priests were forbidden to take part in politics and the Vatican thus clearly distanced itself from political Catholicism. A number of leading figures in the BVP were arrested and on 4 July the party dissolved itself. The Centre Party followed suit the next day.

The regime made quick work of the DNVP. The party leader Hugenberg caused a scandal during the London economic conference in June by demanding the return of Germany's colonies and expansion in the east, thus providing Hitler with an excellent excuse to dismiss him from the cabinet. The *Stahlhelm* leader Franz Seldte demonstrably joined the National Socialists on 26 April and on 21 June the *Stahlhelm* was amalgamated with the SA. On 27 June a 'Friendly Agreement' was reached between the NSDAP and the DNVP. All conservative members of the Reichstag became Nazi party members, and all party members who had been arrested were released. The demise of the DNVP passed almost unnoticed. The Nazi daily newspaper *Völkischer Beobachter* had already announced on 10 June that the 'party state' was dead. On 14 July, a day of particular significance to democrats as the anniversary of the storming of the Bastille, a law was promulgated which declared the NSDAP to be the only legal party in Germany. Goebbels announced that this was the final victory over the ideals of the enlightenment and the French Revolution.

But the regime made provision for plebiscites, thus showing that even dictatorships have, however fraudulent the means, to make some claim to legitimacy by securing popular consent. The spirit of 1789 was thus not quite extinguished.

JULY 1933–AUGUST 1934: THE CONSOLIDATION OF POWER

All professional associations, societies and clubs were brought under party control as part of the comprehensive programme of 'co-ordination' (*Gleichschaltung*). Walter Darré, the party's agricultural expert, author of such works as *On Blood and Soil* and *The New Aristocracy of Blood and Soil*, and a long-time friend of Himmler's, took control over all Germany's farmers' associations and was given the title of 'Reich Farmers' Leader'. He was appointed minister of agriculture at the end of June, and thus had complete control over all aspects of agriculture.

On 1 April the offices of the Reich Association of German Industry (RDI) were raided by the SA and a number of officials were dismissed, among them the vice-president Paul Silverberg who, although he was a Nazi sympathizer, was Jewish. In the following month the RDI was completely reorganized. The name was slightly changed, but the initials remained the same to give the appearance of continuity. Gustav Krupp von Bohlen und Halbach was appointed president who, along with Hjalmar Schacht the former president of the Reichsbank, organized the 'Adolf Hitler Fund' which collected money from industrialists for the NSDAP.

Gleichschaltung affected every walk of life. The professional organizations of doctors, lawyers and engineers were brought under party control and henceforth there were only National Socialist beekeepers' associations and National Socialist cycle clubs. Even village skittles teams were closely watched by the party. As a result, Germany's vigorous and varied club life withered, and people stayed at home or visited the local pub where they learnt to keep an eye out for police informants.

The SA combed local government offices, the banks and department stores in the search for democrats and Jews. A campaign began to drive women out of the professions, the civil service and business, so that they could become the ideal wives and mothers that National Socialism demanded.

In May hundreds of university professors made an open declaration of their devotion to the new regime hoping thereby to further their miserable careers. But it was not only the second-rate who supported Hitler's dictatorship. Martin Heidegger, Germany's greatest philosopher, lauded the regime in a speech given in his capacity of rector of the University of Freiburg. It was a speech that he never retracted, although he was later to find kind words for Hitler's nemesis, Josef Stalin. Carl Schmidt, a renowned expert on constitutional law, provided ingenious justification for Nazi lawlessness. But he soon fell from grace because, unlike the sage of Todtnauberg, he had a wide circle of Jewish friends. This, however, did not stop him from addressing a meeting of German jurists with the words: 'We need to free the German spirit from all Jewish falsifications, falsifications of the concept of spirit which have made it possible for Jewish emigrants to label the great struggle of *Gauleiter* Julius Streicher as something unspiritual.'

The 'Law for the Restoration of a Professional Civil Service' of 7 April 1933 was designed to purge the civil service of Jews and others whom the regime found undesirable. Since university professors were civil servants it was used to rid the universities of a number of prominent intellectuals, many of whom made an incalculable contribution to the countries in which they found asylum. The systematic purge of the universities was carried out by Alfred Rosenberg's 'Battle Group for German Culture' ably assisted by students in the National Socialist German Students' Association.

Having one Jewish grandparent was sufficient to be considered a Jew under the terms of this law, which was soon extended to include the legal profession, doctors, dentists and dental technicians as well as accountants. At Hindenburg's insistence, 'Jewish' civil servants who had been in office before 1 August 1914, who had served in the war, or who had either fathers or sons killed in the war were exempted.

Germany's rich and exciting cultural life was also brought under strict party control. In mid-February the socialist novelist Heinrich Mann was forced to resign as president of the Prussian Academy of the Arts. When the academy was required to make a declaration of loyalty to the regime in March, Heinrich Mann's brother Thomas, along with Ricarda Huch and Alfred Döblin, resigned in protest. Other distinguished writers such as Franz Werfel and Jakob Wassermann were also forced to leave.

In April a long list was published of authors whose works were banned, among whom were Karl Marx, Alfred Einstein, Sigmund Freud and Eduard Bernstein. Heinrich Heine was also banned, but some of his poetry such as 'The Lorelei' was so popular that it was still published. The author was said to be anonymous.

In May the National Socialist German Students' Association organized an 'Action Against the Un–German Spirit'. Bonfires were lit throughout the country into which books and newspapers were thrown. Goebbels addressed the crowds assembled around a huge bonfire in Berlin proclaiming that the intellectual foundations of the November republic had now been destroyed. Heinrich Heine, on witnessing similar book burnings almost a century before, had uttered the prophetic words: 'In the end one burns people where books are burnt.'

The persecution of the Jews, which began in the first weeks of the regime, was carried out in a manner typical of the Nazis. It was a combination of unco-ordinated violence from below and control from above. Bully-boys from the SA went on the rampage vandalizing Jewish property, beating and murdering their hapless victims. Jews from all walks of life fell prey to this ever-increasing wave of violence.

The reaction from abroad was immediate and robust, but this merely provoked the regime to step up its anti-Semitic campaign. Goebbels promised that he would 'teach foreign Jews a lesson' for interfering in German affairs on behalf of their 'racial comrades'. A 'Central Defence Committee Against Jewish Atrocity and Boycott Besetment' was formed under Julius Streicher, the *Gauleiter* of Franconia, an utterly repulsive creature even by the exceptional standards set by the National Socialists, who rejoiced in the reputation of being the movement's most brutal, scatological and vicious anti-Semite. He was rewarded by being given the task of organizing a boycott of Jewish businesses to take place on 1 April.

It was not a success. The SA prevented people from shopping at their favourite stores, and there was widespread complaint about the crude excesses of the Brownshirts. Goebbels was disappointed at the lack of popular enthusiasm for his operation, and promptly called it off. Party activists continued the boycott in some areas, even though both Hitler and Frick had ordered them to stop for fear of foreign reaction.

Within a year 2,000 civil servants had been dismissed and about the same number of artists were forbidden to work. 4,000 lawyers were no longer able to practise their profession, and hundreds of doctors and university professors lost their livelihoods. For the moment Jewish businessmen were needed to help the process of economic recovery, but their days were numbered.

In the first year of the regime some 37,000 German Jews emigrated, even though Jewish agencies only recommended leaving the country if an individual was in extreme personal danger. They hoped that things would calm down, and that it would be possible for the Jewish community to enjoy a degree of autonomy within the new state. It was almost impossible for the Jewish community to believe that worse would befall them. Had not Rabbi Leo Baeck described Germany as witnessing the third golden age of Judaism, following that of Hellenic Judaism in the period before the destruction of the second temple, and that of Sephardic Judaism before the expulsion from Spain? Did the fact that thirteen of the 33 German Nobel Prize winners were Jewish count for nothing? Could the extraordinary contribution of Jews to Germany's cultural heritage simply be ignored? Others were less confident. In 1934 a further 23,000 Jews left the country.

But the optimism of those who stayed was to some extent justified. Things began to settle down in the summer of 1933, by which time Hitler had destroyed the republic and had virtually absolute power. But the military, industry and the bureaucracy still enjoyed a degree of autonomy and Hitler was still partially dependent on them and thus could not afford to go on too radical a course. Hitler was also concerned not to alienate foreign opinion and presented himself as a man of moderation and peace. The Nazis' radicals centred on Ernst Röhm and the SA were deeply frustrated at such pusillanimous behaviour and complained bitterly that there had been no revolutionary changes in German society.

Thus while the SA with about 3 million members was champing at the bit and eager to begin what they called the 'Second Revolution', Hitler was trying to dampen down this radicalism which threatened his fruitful alliance with the old élites. In an attempt to bring the anarchic violence of the SA under control, greater powers were given to Himmler's SS, specialists in orderly, bureaucratic violence infused with ideological passion. The SS established their first concentration camp in a former munitions factory at Dachau near Munich. Here the regime's victims were systematically bullied, tortured and murdered in a secluded camp, without offending the sensitive German public who found the open violence of the SA, to which they had been eyewitnesses, somewhat offensive. At the end of June Himmler appointed SS-*Oberführer* (Brigadier) Theodor Eicke commandant. He was a sadistic brute who had recently been released from a psychiatric hospital for the criminally insane. He immediately began to organize the SS Death's Head units which guarded the camps and was soon to be promoted to inspector general of the concentration camps with his headquarters at the new camp at Sachsenhausen. In October 1933 the SA lost control over their concentration camps which were henceforth administered by the SS, even though the SS was still formally subordinate to the SA.

By the spring of 1934 the conflict between the SA and the Army had become so acute as to be worrisome to Hitler. Ernst Röhm had accused the regime of 'falling asleep' and announced that 'It is high time that the national revolution should become the National Socialist revolution.' At a series of mass meetings he demanded that 'reactionaries' should be weeded out from the bureaucracy, industry and the military. He was outraged that the military had been largely spared from the process of *Gleichschaltung*, but said that its time would come. 'The grey rock of the *Reichswehr*', he proclaimed, 'will disappear beneath the brown wave of the SA.' Hitler could not tolerate such a suggestion. He needed the professionals in the *Reichswehr* and knew full well that he could never fulfil his territorial ambitions with gangs of street-fighting men, whatever their ideological fervour and activist élan. The *Reichswehr* saw Röhm and his *ouvriériste* ideas as a serious danger, and suggested that the SA should form a sort of Territorial Army under its close control. Hitler felt that this solution would probably be unacceptable to Röhm, but decided to test his reactions.

The *Reichswehr* was more than happy to make some concessions to the new regime. The traditionally anti-Semitic officer corps was happy to purge its ranks of Jews. Admittedly this purge was far from complete, largely due to the difficulty in determining who was Jewish. 2,000–3000 'pure Jews' (*Volljuden*) served in the *Wehrmacht* during the war along with 150,000–200,000 'half-Jews' and 'quarter-Jews'. Most served in the ranks, but there were many officers and some 20 generals among them. In February 1934 the swastika was incorporated into military emblems. In the same month Hitler called a meeting between the *Reichswehr* minister General Werner von Blomberg and Röhm and suggested that since the revolution was over and the *Reichswehr* should remain above politics, the SA should restrict its activities to political indoctrination and pre-military training. Hitler told them that a war would have to be fought to secure *Lebensraum* and that war should be left to the professionals. Röhm left the meeting in a towering rage calling Hitler 'an ignorant corporal' and vowing to keep up the struggle against 'reactionaries'. In a speech on 18 April he denounced 'the incredible tolerance' of the regime towards 'the supporters and associates of former and ancient regimes' and demanded that they should be 'ruthlessly removed'.

Although Hitler was still reluctant to act against his old companion-in-arms, Röhm had powerful enemies, and it was not simply the *Reichswehr* that was determined to frustrate his ambitions. Göring, Goebbels and Hess were envious of his position, and Himmler and his associate Heydrich resented the fact that the SS played second fiddle to the SA. The fact that he was a notorious homosexual in a country where homosexuality was an offence under article 175 of the criminal code left him wide open to attack. Göring put together a weighty dossier on Röhm and his numerous homosexual accomplices and catamites. *Reichswehr* intelligence co-operated closely with the National Socialist Security Service (SD) in the search for further material to use against Röhm. It was at this time that Himmler took over control of the Prussian Gestapo and he promptly set them to work on the case.

On 4 June, in an attempt to calm things down, Hitler ordered the entire SA to go on leave for the month of July. Röhm's 'reactionaries' were emboldened by this obvious split among the National Socialists and went on the offensive. Once again Papen was to play a key and characteristically disastrous role. It was obvious that Hindenburg did not have much longer to live and the question of a successor now became of pressing concern. The president had fallen seriously ill in April and had not made a complete recovery. Papen tried to convince Hindenburg to call for the restoration of the monarchy in his will. His aim was to establish a military dictatorship in which the conservative élites would keep the Nazi activists in check.

On 17 June 1934 Papen gave a speech at Marburg University, which had been written for him by Edgar Jung, an ultra-conservative Calvinist lawyer whose hazy notions of 'revolutionary conservatism' were strongly influenced by the muddle-headed corporatist speculations of Othmar Spann. The speech was a forceful expression of the conservative opposition to Hitler. Men who had colluded with the Nazis in the vain belief that they could be tamed now realized that they had made a serious error of judgement and that Hitler had to be removed. It is doubtful whether Papen realized the full implications of the speech that Jung had prepared for him, for it came as a bombshell. It was an outspoken attack on the regime's radicalism, violence and lawlessness. A sharp contrast was drawn between conservative authoritarianism and the 'unnatural totalitarian aspirations of National Socialism'. Dynamism and movement could achieve nothing but chaos, and the 'permanent revolution from below' had to be brought to an end. A firm structure was needed in which the rule of law was respected and state authority unchallenged.

Goebbels promptly banned the publication of this speech, and no mention was made of it on the state radio. Jung was arrested and shortly afterwards murdered along with a number of leading figures in this early conservative resistance to Hitler's dictatorship. Jung's *spiritus rector* Othmar

Spann as an Austrian was temporarily spared. After the *Anschluss* he was brutally mishandled and left virtually blind.

Hitler hastened to visit Hindenburg on his estate at Neudeck in an effort at damage control, but realized that the time had come to take more drastic action. Göring, Himmler and Blomberg decided that the SS should be set loose on the SA leadership, the weapons and logistics to be supplied by the *Reichswehr*. Hitler then called a meeting of senior SA commanders at Bad Wiesee where Röhm was taking the waters. In the early morning of 30 June Hitler arrived at Röhm's hotel in a state of great agitation, riding crop in hand, accompanied by Goebbels and SA-*Obergruppenführer* (General) Viktor Lutze, who was to take over command of the SA, along with an SS detachment. Röhm and his associates were arrested, taken first to the prison at Stadelheim and then transferred to Dachau where they were executed that evening by the SS. Röhm was killed on the following day once Hitler had been finally persuaded to agree to his execution.

This 'Röhm putsch' or 'Night of the Long Knives' was not confined to the SA. A number of old scores were settled. Schleicher, his wife and his adjutant were gunned down in his own home. The former Bavarian prime minister Kahr was assassinated, as was the leader of a prominent Catholic layman's group. Gregor Strasser was dragged off to the cellars of the Gestapo headquarters in the Prinz-Albrecht-Strasse in Berlin where he was shot. A music critic by the name of Dr Wilhelm Schmidt was also murdered, having had the misfortune to be confused with the SA leader Ludwig Schmitt. There were a total of 85 known victims on 30 June, but the real figure is almost certainly considerably higher.

The regime had taken a critical step towards a state of total lawlessness that was characteristic of the fully-fledged Nazi tyranny. Although the state had now degenerated to the level of a criminal organization, there was widespread popular support for this bloodbath. The cabinet was called together on 3 July and hastily cobbled together a law that justified these 'emergency measures' that were needed to combat 'treasonable attacks'. These criminal acts were thus legalized after the event, and no legal action could be taken against the perpetrators. Carl Schmitt opined that 'the *Führer* protects the law from the worst forms of abuse when he uses his position as leader to create the law in his capacity as supreme judge'. He was later to extend this dubious definition of the law in the lapidary injunction that 'the will of the *Führer* is the highest law'.

Most Germans were relieved that the SA with their brutal activism had now been brought under control by Hitler's decisive action. They forgot that law and order could not be restored by murderous disregard for the law. Even though two prominent generals had been slaughtered in cold blood, the *Reichswehr* was delighted that the SA had been silenced and the generals cravenly congratulated Hitler for saving Germany from the horrors of civil war. Hitler had thus overcome all serious opposition within the Nazi movement and his dazzling position as the omniscient and omnipotent *Führer* in the eyes of his countless devotees was further enhanced.

The cabinet met as President Hindenburg lay dying and it was agreed that on his demise Hitler should combine the offices of chancellor and president. None of those present were troubled that this was blatantly unconstitutional and flouted the Enabling Act. Blomberg toadyishly announced that on the Field Marshal's death he would order the *Reichswehr* to make a personal oath of allegiance to the *Führer* rather than to the constitution as had previously been the case. A number of soldiers were thus to suffer severe and genuine pangs of conscience when they contemplated resistance to the man to whom before Almighty God they had sworn total allegiance. Blomberg vainly imagined that the oath of allegiance would guarantee their independence. They were soon to find out that the absolute reverse was true.

three
THE NATIONAL SOCIALIST STATE
2 August 1934–1 September 1939

THE NATIONAL SOCIALIST STATE

Hindenburg died on 2 August 1934 and Hitler was promptly appointed '*Führer* and Reich Chancellor'. The dictatorship was now complete. On 19 August a plebiscite was held asking the German people to approve the appointment of Hitler as head of state, chancellor, supreme commander of the armed forces and head of the judiciary, thus giving pseudo-democratic sanction to a blatantly unconstitutional move. 89.9 per cent voted in favour. On the following day Hitler announced that the 'fifteen-year struggle for power' was completed and that the National Socialists now controlled everything from the highest offices in the Reich to the smallest village council. This was no idle boast. All aspects of German life were now firmly under party control. At the beginning of September the sixth party rally was held in Nuremberg to celebrate this astonishing victory. Its pomp, ceremony and menace was captured on celluloid in Leni Riefenstahl's brilliant piece of propaganda, *Triumph of the Will*.

The film's title, whether deliberately or not, is misleading. Hitler did not owe his success to his iron willpower, but to a set of fortunate circumstances that offered him opportunities that he exploited adroitly. He gambled for very high stakes and luck smiled upon him. The social, economic and political crises created a situation in which a firm hand was needed. Men of power and influence imagined that they could use the little drummer boy for their own purposes while the National Socialist movement developed an anarchic activist dynamic that swept all before it. Hitler the master tactician managed to stop the situation from getting out of hand,

and thereby won the allegiance of the conservative élites who felt most threatened by party radicals. This was no carefully considered plan carried out with ruthless determination, but eighteen months of breathless improvisation and nerve-wracking risk.

The rule of law no longer applied. Parliamentary democracy had been destroyed, the separation of powers ended, the constitution was defunct, the federal system dismantled and a number of new bodies created that were answerable neither to the state nor to the party, but alone to Hitler. Conservatives believed that with the destruction of the radicals in the SA the regime would now settle down to be firmly repressive yet predictably authoritarian, and that the road ahead would be smooth.

Once again the conservative élites had seriously misread the situation. They failed to see that behind the façade of unity there were ferocious struggles for power, conflicts over areas of competence and bitter rivalries. The system was in a constant state of flux and possessed an inner dynamic without which it would atrophy. It was unpredictable, anarchic and individualistic in that the little *Führers* called the shots and were not bound by rules, regulations or the law. Officials tried to interpret Hitler's will, for that was the highest law and the secret of success. The resulting situation was so chaotic that during the war Hitler's closest associate, Martin Bormann, complained that, whereas the Republic had been far too tightly bound with red tape, the present situation was so disorderly as to be dysfunctional. A highly complex modern state could not possibly function effectively by attempts to interpret the wishes of an individual, particularly when the leader became progressively unhinged as the war dragged on and his will became little more than wishful thinking. Furthermore many of the leading figures in the Third Reich were exceedingly idle and absurdly vain. In the latter stages of the war Göring spent most of the year hunting and playing with his electric trains in his vast palace Karinhall. Wilhelm Frick relaxed in his lakeside home on the Chiemsee. Philip Bouhler, who ran Hitler's personal chancellery, idled away for months on end at his country estate in Nussdorf.

Hitler was indubitably the fount of all authority and the final arbiter, but his unbridled power did not rest solely on his willpower, and certainly not on his careful planning, but rather on the inner workings of the system and the willingness of so many Germans to lend him their support and devotion.

The years from 1934 to 1938 appeared to be a time of tranquillity and peace in Germany. The regime was authoritarian, but it seemed to have distanced itself from the radical activism of the 'Years of Struggle'. It had a number of striking successes to its credit, both at home and abroad. A comprehensive welfare state was created and the feeling of 'racial community' (*Volksgemeinschaft*) was more than an empty slogan. It was not only in Germany that Hitler was seen as a man of peace who had restored Germany to its rightful place in the world.

Behind the scenes the situation was very different. Hitler was systematically laying the groundwork for the realization of his schemes for conquest, expansion and racial purification. Many in the military, civil service and industrial élite, to say nothing of the people at large, agreed in principle with these aims, but they feared the risks involved. Hitler needed first to bring them totally under his control and bend them to his will before he put all his chips on the table in one desperate *va banque* gamble. It was to be total victory or total destruction – Hitler would brook no alternative.

By August 1934 Hitler had absolute power. In the state there was no body or person who could check or control him. With the removal of Ernst Röhm he had unbridled authority over the party, which followed him blindly. Hitler as *Führer* was the awesome figure that bound this confusing and fissiparous movement together, and Goebbels' brilliant propaganda helped make him into a figure of messianic proportions, the superbly choreographed rallies becoming quasi-religious ceremonies.

This could not have been done purely with smoke and mirrors, nor could the German people's longing for a saviour in their hour of need be stilled without results. The regime overcame the unemployment problem, stimulated the economy and had a series of foreign political successes that silenced most of Hitler's critics and reconciled the masses to the countless irritations of daily life. Hitler was credited with all the many successes; the failures were ascribed to his wretched underlings.

Initially the élites believed that they could tame Hitler, or where they were unable to do so to profit from him. They were reassured by the fact that for a little while he played by the book as written by Brüning and Papen. But he quickly dropped established governmental routine. The cabinet met 72 times in 1933, 12 times in 1935 and not at all after 1938, so that the vast cabinet room in Hitler's magnificent new Reich chancellery was never used. At none of these cabinet meetings was a vote taken. Members of the cabinet met Hitler individually, access to the Presence being controlled by his assiduous head of chancellery, Hans Heinrich Lammers.

Once the Enabling Act was passed, Hitler's working methods became even more haphazard. When he was not rushing around the country addressing rallies, laying foundation stones, and calling impromptu meetings with sundry officials, he paid increasingly long visits to the Berghof, his mountain fastness in Berchtesgaden. Officials scurried around after him begging for his approval. The result was inevitably chaotic. One minister would secure his endorsement of legislation that contradicted that which had already been passed via another ministry. All this further strengthened Hitler's position as *Führer*, for he alone could reconcile such differences and order the implementation of laws so as to create the impression of order and consistency.

Hitler resisted all attempts to bring some order into this confusion which exasperated the orderly minds of experienced bureaucrats. His instructions were often deliberately vague, so that many different interpretations were possible as to how they should be executed. Or he hesitated until one of his powerful subordinates took it upon himself to act. Amid this tangled situation there was plenty of room for ambitious *Gauleiter* and *Reichsstatthälter* to carve out empires where they reigned supreme, virtually unhampered by considerations of the law or of established practice, and with a direct line of communication to Hitler. Since Hitler took little interest in domestic politics in these early years, there was ample scope for power-hungry and resourceful men to establish themselves in positions of authority and influence, and they could be almost certain of the *Führer's* blessing. In National Socialist Germany nothing succeeded like success.

Hitler seldom intervened and ruled at a distance. The shortcomings and failures of the regime could thus be blamed on local party functionaries, and did nothing to undermine his status as the nation's redeemer. On the contrary: 'If only the *Führer* knew' was a frequent response to the widespread irritations, injustices and deficiencies.

The longing for a leader who would deliver Germany from all evil was deeply rooted both ideologically and psychologically. There was the emperor Frederick I of Hohenstaufen who as 'Barbarossa' lay buried in the Kyffhäuser mountain and who would rise again to save Germany in its hour of need. There were the Parsifals and Siegfrieds in Wagner's operas that Hitler loved so dearly. There was the deeply ingrained military spirit of Brandenburg-Prussia, the leadership ideology of the youth movement, and the widespread desire to find a substitute for the monarchy as a symbolic representation of the nation. But it was Goebbels and his propaganda machine who transformed admiration of the regime's achievements into a quasi-religious cult of the *Führer*. 'The whole *Volk*,' he proclaimed, 'is devoted to him not merely through respect, but with deep and heartfelt love, because it has the feeling that it belongs to Him. It is flesh of his flesh, blood of his blood.' Perhaps only someone who had been educated by Jesuits could be capable of such blasphemy.

Few were able to resist enchantment by this superhuman figure. Erstwhile opponents became his devotees, and even those who remained critically distanced from him found it hard to withstand his attraction. Hitler himself succumbed totally to the myth so that this mean-spirited, cruel, and bigoted creature became convinced that he was an infallible and indispensable instrument of providence, with a world-historical mission to fulfil. Those who even today speak of the 'fascination' of the Hitler phenomenon are still under the spell of this despicable megalomaniac.

As early as 1940 the émigré social scientist Ernst Fraenkel described this confusion of rival power centres in the state and the party as the 'Dual State' and another brilliant colleague, Franz Neumann, analysed how the normative state apparatus gradually dissolved into an 'organized anarchy' with its characteristically amorphous dynamic. The dualism was not a clear-cut distinction between party and state, but a highly complex intertwining of areas of competence which led to ever-increasingly radicalization both of goals and methods.

There were substantial changes within the power structure of this poly-cratic state. The SS triumphed over the SA in 1934 and began its rapid growth to become a state within the state, submitting the judiciary and the police to its whims. Walter Darré, although grossly inefficient, was made 'food tsar' and minister of agriculture with extensive powers. The German Work Front (DAF) built on the ruins of the democratic unions under Robert Ley, a chronic alcoholic, had 25.3 million members by 1939. This gave Ley immense power which he used to tackle questions of professional training, social problems, housing and leisure-time activities. His empire thus infringed at many points on the competence of other ministries. Similarly, Fritz Todt was made responsible for building the highways and given special plenipotentiary powers that enabled him to tread on the toes of a number of ministers, principal among them the minister of transport. One of these ministers was the founder of the *Stahlhelm*, Franz Seldte, a bone-idle creature who had been appointed minister of labour in 1933. When Goebbels suggested to Hitler that Ley should replace Seldte, on the grounds that although he was an appalling drunk he tended to get things done, Hitler refused point blank. He argued that Seldte could always be removed, whereas Ley was in a position of such power and influence that it would be extremely difficult to dislodge him. The situation was made even more absurd in that, as Ernst Jünger pointed out, none of these magnates would have even been made a junior partner in a halfway decent firm.

No one accumulated so many offices as the intelligent, jovial, sadistic, morphine-addicted and progressively deranged Göring. He was president of the Reichstag, Prussian minister of the interior, and Prussian prime minister. He was a Reich minister without portfolio, air minister, minister responsible for hunting and the forests, commander-in-chief of the Luftwaffe, and commissar for raw materials and foreign exchange. When Hitler decided to push ahead with his autarky plans in spite of the resistance of the central bank, the ministry of economics and powerful voices in the private sector, he appointed Göring head of the Four Year Plan and as such virtual dictator over all aspects of the economy.

Goebbels combined the office of Minister of Propaganda with that of *Gauleiter* of Berlin. Bernhard Rust, the *Gauleiter* of Hanover and Braunschweig, was also minister of technology and education, even though he had lost his job as a schoolteacher after sexually abusing one his charges. He also suffered from a severe mental handicap as a result of a head wound received while serving as an infantry lieutenant during the war. Rust and Goebbels were the only *Gauleiter* who were also ministers.

Heinrich Himmler was both head of the SS and police chief for all of Germany. In October 1939 he was made 'Reich Commissar for the Strengthening of the German Race (*Volkstum*)'. As such he was responsible for the brutal deportation of Jews and Poles, and the resettlement by pure-blooded Germans of the areas they had been forced to leave. This new office as a 'Higher Instance of the Reich' was placed outside the law and kept secret from the regular civil service. Himmler also became minister of the interior in 1943 and was given command over the reserve army in the following year.

Some held positions of great power without holding state office. Julius Streicher, the grisly *Gauleiter* of Franconia, enjoyed Hitler's absolute and unconditional support for his rabidly pornographic and sadistic anti-Semitism. Baldo von Shirach as head of the Hitler Youth (HJ) and later Reich Youth Leader was another powerful figure, in spite of his widely rumoured homosexuality and his endless struggles with Bernhard Rust.

Hitler was obsessed with architecture and had megalomanic plans for rebuilding Berlin. When he felt that planning was not going ahead fast enough he appointed an ambitious young architect, Albert Speer, 'General Building Inspector for the Reich Capital'; this office gave him plenipotentiary powers over building and traffic. Speer was appointed minister of munitions on Todt's death in an aeroplane crash in February 1942.

Meanwhile the traditional ministries continued to work as before so that an impression of normality was created amid all this chaos. The party had become a gigantic bureaucratized apparatus with 700,000 well-paid employees by 1937. It nearly trebled in size during the war as the 'golden pheasants', as these gold-braided officials were caustically called, found ingenious ways to avoid dying a hero's death for *Führer und Vaterland*.

Party officials down to the very lowest had the means to make the lives of ordinary people miserable, and many took great delight in doing so. The Party Wards (*Ortsgruppen*) were obliged to provide certificates of good conduct for civil servants, for those who requested social assistance, and for students and apprentices. No business could be started without the sanction of the party and during the war it was the party that decided which workers were essential and therefore exempted from military service. The Block Leader (*Blockleiter*) kept a close watch on the citizenry and extracted contributions from them for party membership, the National Socialist People's Welfare (NSV) as well as for the 'Winter Help' (*Winterhilfswerk*). These Nazi charitable organizations amounted to little more than state-sponsored mugging, and a large chunk of the proceeds went to build Goebbels' magnificent villa in Berlin. Money was also collected through 'Casserole Sundays' whereby the proceeds of a modest one-course meal went to assist needy 'racial comrades'. During the war the *Blockleiter* issued ration cards. The opportunities for harassment were unlimited, and complaints about these vile mini-Hitlers at the bottom of the Nazi midden were legion.

The most spectacular change since 1934 was the rise of the SS to become the purest expression of National Socialism. It had begun as a minute subordinate section of the SA, but by 1933 it had 56,000 members. Himmler began to build up his police empire in Bavaria, but the way ahead was blocked by Göring who controlled the police in Prussia. There began a bitter personal rivalry between the two men with strong ideological overtones. Göring saw the police as an organ of the state, Himmler wanted a political police force that was completely free from any form of outside control and utterly devoted to the *Führer*.

Heinrich Himmler was an improbable leader of this new order of ideologically charged Aryan supermen. He was a weedy and shy little man, born in 1900, who did not lose his virginity until 1928. In gratitude for this act of mercy he promptly married his dreary Jezebel, temporarily retired from political life and took up chicken farming. Although unsuccessful with the poultry he channelled his agricultural expertise into an obsession with breeding and with race. His devotion to Hitler was unconditional.

The SS (*Schutzstaffel* – Guard Squad) was founded in 1923 under a slightly different name, and was reorganized in 1925. Himmler took over command of its 289 members in 1929 and set to work turning it into an élite formation. In 1931 he established the Security Service (SD) under the unrelentingly malevolent 25-year-old Reinhard Heydrich, a racial fanatic who had recently been dismissed from the navy for dishonourable conduct. Shortly after the March elections the first military formation was created known as the 'SS Personal Standard Adolf Hitler' (*Leibstandarte*-SS *Adolf Hitler*) under the command of Sepp Dietrich, a former butcher and bouncer whose coarseness was only partially concealed behind a heavy layer of beer-swilling Bavarian joviality. After the SS' victory over the SA, the first units of the SS-*Verfügungstruppe* (Emergency Troops) were formed, which were later to be reorganized into the *Waffen*-SS, the military wing. On 20 June 1934 the SS was made solely responsible for the concentration camps which were guarded by the SS Death's Head Units (SS-*Totenkopfverbände*).

By the spring of 1934 Himmler had taken over the political police forces in all the German states with the exception of Prussia. Göring, who was looking for an ally in the interminable power-struggles that beset the Third Reich, decided to make his peace with Himmler and gave him control over the Prussian secret police, the Gestapo, in April 1934. Himmler was now in control of the secret police throughout the Reich and placed Heydrich in command. Heydrich was now head of the SD and the Gestapo, and thus of both the party and the state secret police forces. In 1936 the Gestapo was made independent from judicial and administrative control. Himmler was now given command over all the regular police forces in Germany and sported the pompous title of '*Reichsführer*-SS and Chief of the German Police in the Reich Ministry of the Interior'.

In a situation typical of the Third Reich, Himmler was thus subordinate to the minister of the interior in his capacity as state secretary in charge of the police, but as head of the SS he reported directly to Hitler. With immediate access to the *Führer* he could afford to ignore the minister of the interior, and the entire police force was thus beyond state control. Himmler did not see fit to even have an office in the ministry of the interior.

Himmler immediately began the reorganization of his all-encompassing empire. The police was divided into two sections. The Order Police (*Ordnungspolizei*), which dealt with minor offences, comprised the Safety Police (*Schutzpolizei*) and the *Gendarmerie* and was commanded by Kurt Daluege, a Freikorps veteran and early party member, a man of such limited intelligence that he was popularly known as *Dummi-Dummi*. Heydrich was put in charge of the Security Police (*Sicherheitspolizei*) made up of the Political Police, the Criminal Police (*Kripo*) and the Border Police. In September 1939 the party's secret police force, the SD, was added to the *Sicherheitspolizei* to form the Reich Security Main Office (RSHA).

Heydrich was determined to turn the SS into 'ideological storm-troopers and bodyguards of the *Führer's* ideas'. Its mission was to 'keep a close eye on the political health of the body politic (*Volkskörper*), quickly diagnose any symptoms of sickness and to immediately destroy all malignant cells'. Himmler told his men that they had to steel themselves to face 'the campaign of annihilation of Germany's subhuman enemies throughout the entire world' which he would soon unleash.

Heydrich's RSHA was divided up into numerous divisions to combat the regime's enemies and ill-wishers. There were sections dealing with such issues as communism, Marxism and its allies, reactionary movements, opposition groups, legitimists, liberalism, political Catholicism and Protestantism, sects and Freemasons, abortion, homosexuality and racial research. Section IV B 4 was given responsibility for questions concerning 'Political Churches, Sects and Jews'. Its head was SS-*Obersturmbannführer* (Lieutenant-Colonel) Adolf Eichmann. Section IV C dealt with those unfortunates in 'protective custody', Section IV D with foreign workers and hostile foreigners; Section VII with 'ideological research and evaluation'.

As early as 1934 Heydrich made his intentions perfectly clear. He announced that 'the aim of our Jewish policy (*Judenpolitik*) must be emigration of all Jews'. He then added an even more sinister note: 'Rowdy anti-Semitism must be rejected. One does not fight rats with revolvers, but with poison and gas.'

The SS was thus a totalitarian organization designed to protect the German *Volk*, rid it of all undesirable elements whether biological or ideological, and thus render it pure, strong and healthy. Heinrich Himmler, the prim little bureaucrat known as the 'Reich Heini', was a mass of contradictions. He was a merciless mass murderer who found a visit to Auschwitz disturbing and tried to ban hunting on the grounds that it was cruel to animals. He used every modern technique in order to extirpate the evil works of Jewish–Bolshevik subhumans and create his atavistic dystopia, but he was full of anxieties and fears about the modern world. He wanted to turn the SS into a mystical order, living in remote castles, worshipping the ancient Germanic gods, abjuring alcohol and tobacco and adhering to a strictly vegetarian diet.

In order to hunt down and destroy the enemies of the *Volk* the regime undermined and eventually destroyed the rule of law. The law could not remain independent in a totalitarian regime, but was instrumentalized to serve its needs. Special courts were opened in each state against the decisions of which there could be no appeal. There were a number of new criminal offences, such as 'Acts Contrary to the Healthy Feelings of the *Volk*', which were open to a wide range of interpretations. The concept of the rule of law was denounced as 'liberal' and was replaced by such notions as 'the will of the *Führer* is the highest law', or 'law is that which is good for the *Volk*'.

Whereas civil law was administered in much the same way as before, the courts outbid one another in the ferocity of their judgements in criminal cases. Members of the Communist and Social Democratic parties were ruthlessly pursued and charged with treason. Merely listening to Radio Moscow, or the BBC during the war, was considered to be 'preparation for treason'. 16,000 death sentences had been handed down for such offenses by the end of 1944. The courts also interpreted questions of 'racial law' with exceptional ideological fervour.

With the Gestapo law of February 1936 the individual citizen was left without any legal protection whatsoever. The Gestapo could define what constituted a political crime and the courts had no jurisdiction over its activities. If the Gestapo did not approve of the judgement of a court they would simply arrest the accused and fling the hapless individual into a concentration camp. Roland Freisler, state secretary in the ministry of justice and later president of the People's Court, a sadistic former Communist commissar, threatened to deliver any judges who handed down light sentences to this 'police justice'. The law became even more draconian during the war with a host of new capital offences such as 'taking advantage of the state of war'.

RACISM AND ANTI-SEMITISM: THE FIRST PHASE

The persecution of the Jews provides the paradigmatic example of the lawlessness, ideological fervour and ruthless brutality of the Nazi tyranny.

It was also characteristic of the regime that it should be part of a process of gradual radicalization, and that it should be carried out in a somewhat haphazard way as various power-centres within this polycratic system vied with one another. The very notion of the 'racial community' is by definition exclusive, and from the beginning the Nazis spoke of their determination to destroy everything that was deemed to be 'alien to the community' (*Gemeinschaftsfremd*) in order to hasten the creation of a pure, healthy and superior race. The National Socialist concept of law was based on the will of the *Führer* and on the 'healthy instincts of the *Volk*'; thus all who were outside the *Volk* were also outside the law. Although Jews were seen as the greatest danger to the *Volk,* other groups were also singled out for exclusion. These included the mentally and physically handicapped, psychiatric patients, male homosexuals, gypsies, habitual criminals, alcoholics, drug addicts and other 'asocials'. This in spite of the fact that most of the leading figures in Nazi Germany fell under one or more of these categories, with the possible exception of the gypsies. These latter were damned on three counts. They were deemed to be 'asocial', 'inferior', and 'racially unacceptable' (*Fremdrassig*). In Berlin Goebbels declared Jews also to be 'asocial', but it was difficult to charge this sinisterly powerful and deeply threatening people with 'inferiority'. Lesbians were only persecuted in Austria where, under paragraphs 129 and 130 of the criminal code, their proclivity was condemned as an 'unnatural sexual offence'. Unlike the Jews, homosexuals were not systematically hunted down and murdered, and there was an extensive homosexual sub-culture in the Third Reich. In the early years many homosexuals were attracted by the markedly homoerotic aesthetic of the 'Movement', and a number of leading Nazis would have been in serious trouble had paragraph 175 of the criminal code been rigorously enforced.

Compulsory sterilization of the 'hereditarily sick' began in July 1933. A total of about 360,000 such operations were performed. Initially those suffering from such disorders as schizophrenia, epilepsy, manic depression and 'idiocy' were singled out, but soon social rather than medical criteria were more often used. Habitual criminals, alcoholics, prostitutes and tramps were also sterilized in this extensive programme of 'racial hygiene'. The Nazis first decided what was 'normal' and then set about destroying everything that did not match these criteria in a desperate attempt to build a new society.

The regime moved a little more cautiously in 1934 since it was preoccupied with the Röhm crisis and was concerned to improve its image abroad. The attack was now concentrated on the handicapped and those suffering from hereditary conditions. As an initial precaution they were forced to undergo compulsory sterilization in order to avoid further damage to the genetic stock.

Julius Streicher stepped up his personal anti-Semitic campaign in his obscene publication *Der Stürmer* which was put on public display in showcases throughout Germany from the summer of 1934. He demanded that Jews should be denied all civil rights and that marriages between Jews and Gentiles should be forbidden. In a number of instances registrars refused to allow such marriages, and appeals to the courts against such illegal actions were often in vain.

In 1935 Jews were forbidden to serve in the armed forces. Attempts to create a special nationality law for Jews failed because there was no agreement on how to define who was Jewish. Should 'half-Jews', those with only one Jewish parent, be treated the same as 'full-Jews', both of whose parents were Jewish? Hitler demanded clarification so that further discrimination against Jews could be put in train and 'mixed marriages' outlawed. There had been a revival of 'rowdy anti-Semitism' in 1935 as a result of dissatisfaction among the ranks of the SA at the regime's refusal to carry out a National Socialist revolution. This had hurt Germany's reputation abroad and was bad for business. Consequently there was widespread disapproval of such lawlessness. Most important of all Hitler could not tolerate such insubordination from this dissident rabble. Anti-Semitism had to become a government monopoly and to this end officials from Frick's ministry of the interior worked feverishly during the Nuremberg party rally drafting the 'Law for the Protection of German Blood and German Honour', otherwise known as the 'Nuremberg laws'.

The laws made marriages and sexual intercourse between Jews and non-Jews criminal offences. Jews were forbidden to employ female non-Jews as domestic servants. Only those German citizens who had 'German or similar blood' could enjoy full civil rights. The thorny question of the definition of a Jew was still left open. After lengthy debates it was decided that a Jew was someone who had 'three grandparents who were racially full Jews', a practising Jew with only two Jewish grandparents or someone with two Jewish grandparents who was married to a Jew. Those who only had two Jewish grandparents were dubbed 'Jewish half-breeds' but for the time being still retained their civil rights. Also in 1935 the 'Law for the Protection of the Hereditary Health of the German People' made it impossible for people with hereditary diseases to marry.

Although the Nazis insisted that the Jews were a race they were thus obliged to use religious criteria for deciding who was Jewish. A grotesque and tragic exception was in the Crimea where Otto Ohlendorf, a brilliant academic economist turned mass-murderer, ordered his *Einsatzgruppe* D to kill 6,000 Tartar Krimshaks whom racial experts certified as Jewish. The Turkic Karaimen, who practiced a heterodox form of Judaism, were spared. But other factors played an important role in this bizarre episode. The Karaimen had fought with the Whites in the Civil War, whereas the Krimshaks supported the Bolsheviks. For some equally bizarre reason Portuguese Jews were also deemed to be Aryans.

The Nuremberg laws were something of a compromise and did not satisfy the more radical anti-Semites in the party. Although the Nazis continued to insist that Jews were a race, with these two exceptions the definition of who was Jewish was based solely on religious affiliation. It did not occur to the hordes of crackpot racial researchers and skull-measurers that there could be no other definition.

Jews had already been excluded from the civil service and the professions, and by 1938 60 per cent of Jewish businesses had been confiscated. The once-prosperous Jewish community was now poverty-stricken and subjected to never-ending humiliation and chicanery. In April 1938 they were forced to make a full disclosure of their assets. In July they were given special identity cards. In August they were obliged to add the first names Sarah or Israel and their passports stamped with a 'J'. German Jews thus lost their individual identity, a fact that was further underlined by the Nazi habit of referring to the Jews as 'the Jew' (*der Jude*). In November Jewish children were forbidden to attend state schools.

The fresh wave of radical anti-Semitism in 1938 was particularly strong in Berlin where Goebbels announced that the capital would soon be 'uncontaminated by Jews' (*Judenrein*). He told a meeting of 300 policemen that: 'Law is not the order of the day, but harassment.' In the summer, synagogues and Jewish shops were ransacked and the appallingly corrupt police chief, Count Helldorf, proved most co-operative with the Nazi thugs. In addition to ordering his men to make life as unpleasant as possible for Berlin's Jews, he amassed a vast fortune by confiscating the passports of rich Jews and selling them back for 250,000 marks apiece. Later he was to see the writing on the wall, joined the conspirators of 20 July 1944, was tortured and hanged.

The SD now decided upon a policy of 'ordered harassment' (*geordnetes Schikanieren*). This involved local bans on Jews from visiting public parks, theatres, cinemas and the like. With very few exceptions Jews were banned from practising medicine, the law and similar professions. This placed the Nazis in a bind: on the one hand they wanted the Jews to leave Germany, on the other they had reduced them to such a state of poverty that they were unable to bear the cost of emigration. Violence, as in Austria, now seemed an attractive alternative.

On 7 November 1938 Ernst von Rath, a diplomat serving in the German embassy in Paris, was assassinated by a young Polish-German Jew by the name of Herschel Grynszpan. It was an act of revenge for the gross mistreatment of his parents by the Gestapo. They were among the 75,000 Polish Jews expelled from Germany whom the Poles refused citizenship. A few obtained passages to America; the majority were interned. Rath died on 9 November, the anniversary of Hitler's putsch in Munich where the party leadership was assembled for the yearly celebrations. A 'spontaneous expression of popular outrage' was carefully organized by Goebbels on Hitler's orders, and the *Gauleiter* let loose the SA in a nationwide pogrom euphemistically known as 'The Night of Broken Glass' (*Reichskristallnacht*).

It was a night of shattered lives and broken hopes in which some 100 Jews were brutally murdered, several hundred synagogues burnt to the ground and countless Jewish stores, apartments and houses ransacked. 30,000 Jewish men were arrested and shipped off to concentration camps. That same night Himmler spoke in apocalyptic terms of a war to the death between Germans and Jews.

The majority of Germans averted their gaze while disapproving of the SA rowdies who reminded them of the bad old days of Nazi violence, and expressing their horror at the material damage that had been done. Some were concerned about the reaction from abroad. Precious few helped the unfortunate victims of this outrage.

The 250,000 Jews who still remained in Germany were fined 1,000 million marks for the damage done by the SA and Göring seized the proceeds of all the insurance claims. Finally all remaining Jewish stores and businesses were 'Aryanized'. They were confiscated by the state and sold off to non-Jews at well below their market value. Throughout the Reich all Jews were now forbidden to go to the theatre, the cinema or to public swimming pools. They were thus excluded from German society and barely able to exist.

There were clear indications that even worse was to come. The official SS magazine, *Schwarze Korps*, called for the 'extinction' and the 'total anni-hilation' of this 'parasitic race'. On 12 November Göring told a meeting of senior officials that in the event of a war Germany would 'first of all settle accounts with the Jews'. 9 November 1938 thus marked the end of the phase of pogrom anti-Semitism and the beginning of a bureaucratized and systematic approach to a 'final solution'. The Nazis had by now decided that 'harassment' was not enough: more drastic measures were needed.

ECONOMIC POLICY

Hitler had promised to put Germany back to work, and he was true to his word. Within four years unemployment had been virtually overcome, and some sectors were now short of skilled labour. He benefited from programmes that had already been put in train by the Papen and Schleicher administrations, but the National Socialists set about them with exceptional energy and determination. Plans for a network of highways (*Autobahnen*) had already been laid, but Hitler gave this programme top priority. 1,700 million marks were invested in road building, thus providing employment for thousands and scoring a major propaganda victory. A further 1,300 million was invested in housing and 1,000 million in government buildings. From 1936 armaments were given top priority, so that expenditure on weapons increased from 720 million marks in 1933 to 10,800 million in 1937. In the six peacetime years the government spent the staggering sum of 90,000 million marks on armaments.

Expenditure on this scale could not be covered by revenue or offset by the six-month compulsory labour service, which was introduced in 1935. At first the regime used the same methods as Papen and Schleicher, who had financed their Keynesian schemes by bills of exchange. In May 1933 four large companies, Krupp, Siemens, the Gutehoffnungshütte and Rheinmetall, pooled their resources and formed the Metallurgical Research Association (Mefo) with a capital of 1,000 million marks. The government paid for armaments orders given to these four companies with five-year promissory notes guaranteed by the government and known as Mefo Bills. The government then discounted them so that the Mefo Bills acted as a form of currency.

Mefo Bills worth thousands of millions of marks thus fell due in 1938 and the government took recourse to highly dubious methods in order to pay the bill. Tax relief was offered in lieu of payment, banks were forced to buy government bonds and the government took money from savings accounts and insurance companies. In 1937 the central bank was no longer able to control the volume of money in circulation so that the government used the printing press to meet the cash shortage.

The Nazis put Germany back to work, but the condition of the working class was still wretched. A report in September 1935 showed that almost half of German workers earned less than 18 marks per week, which was below the poverty level. Nationwide the standard of living was still below that of 1928. Food prices were rising rapidly, placing further strain on low-income families.

Concentration on rearmament meant that the government soon faced an acute shortage of foreign exchange and consequently a severe shortage of raw materials. Schacht's 'New Plan' of 1934 introduced strict currency controls but did little to stem the persistent drain on reserves. The Four Year Plan of 1936 which was designed to overcome these problems placed the economy under strict government control and aimed at autarky. Synthetic rubber and substitute fuel was produced on a vast scale and domestic ores exploited in an attempt to lessen dependence on foreign suppliers. Once again the party took the helm, with Göring as a virtual economic dictator setting the course. Two *Gauleiter*, Walter Köhler and Adolf Wagner, were made responsible respectively for the allocation of raw materials and for setting prices. Senior officers in Göring's Luftwaffe were put in charge of oil and energy. Carl Krauch from IG Farben was given plenipotentiary powers over the chemical industries, but he succeeded in keeping it firmly in private hands. Hjalmar Schacht felt that this approach to Germany's pressing economic problems was disastrous and ceased to be minister of economics in 1937. He left the *Reichsbank* two years later.

Just as Schacht had predicted, the autarky programme was an expensive failure. Vast amounts of capital were invested in the Buna and Leuna works near Halle, but Germany was still dependent on foreign supplies of rubber and oil. Domestic iron ore was of very inferior quality and was extremely expensive to mine and smelt and half of the iron ore still had to be imported. Germany was also dependent on imports of manganese, chrome and wolfram, and was still far from self-sufficient in foodstuffs.

The regime tried to produce both guns and butter, but armaments took precedence over consumer goods. By the summer of 1935 industrial production and employment was back at the 1928 level and there was no longer any need to prime the pump. The problems that beset the economy were now almost solely due to excessive government expenditure on armaments, and thus, in spite of the remarkable economic recovery between 1933 and 1939, life remained very austere. In 1938 meat consumption was still below the 1929 level and there was a shortage of quality consumer goods. The average German was happy to have a job but there were an increasing number of complaints about food shortages and the paucity of the better things in life. Industrial wages did not reach the 1928 levels until 1941, and then largely because of long hours of overtime rather than increases in the basic wages.

Early experiments with National Socialist unions were hastily dropped. Known as 'National Socialist Works Cell Organizations' (NSBO), they attracted disaffected left-wing elements who had the temerity to try to further the interests of the membership. In the summer of 1933 'Trustees of Labour' were appointed by the ministry of labour to determine wages, contracts and working conditions. Since these officials were mostly recruited from management they looked after the interests of the employers rather than those of the employees.

Robert Ley was obliged to purge the German Labour Front (DAF) of all those who hoped to create National Socialist unions and now concentrated on the educational programmes and leisure time activities run by 'Strength Through Joy' (KdF). This vast organization, founded in November 1933, offered further education courses, theatrical performances, concerts, sports, holidays at home and abroad, and even cruises.

The DAF was thus rendered totally docile and workers no longer had any voice in management. In November 1933 Gustav Krupp von Bohlen und Halbach agreed that businessmen should be included in the DAF. In the following year the DAF was reorganized with four 'pillars': blue collar workers, white collar workers, industrialists and small businessmen. It had 40,000 full-time staff plus 1.3 million volunteers. 1.5 per cent of workers' wages was deducted to cover costs.

The concessions that had been made to labour during the Weimar Republic were all revoked and a businessman was now master in his own house. The 'leadership principle' (*Führerprinzip*) now applied in the business world. The 'Works *Führer*' ruled supreme over the 'Works Community'. When members of various factory councils complained about this denial of all workers' rights in 1935 the council members were no longer elected but appointed by the Trustees. Workers were now issued with 'Labour Books', which drastically curtailed their freedom of movement from one place of employment to another.

The peasantry was the darling of the Nazi propagandists, the 'biological kernel' of Germany's future greatness, where 'blood and soil' were one. They were susceptible to such flattery and flocked to the Nazi cause, but once the Nazis were in power these rural workers were treated in much the same way as industrial workers. Walter Darré's 'Reich Food Department' (*Reichsnährstand*) exercised dominion over its 17 million members. It was a mammoth bureaucratic organization that, hydra-like, touched all aspects of rural life. It controlled production, prices, and marketing of all agricultural products. It made desperate but vain attempts to bind the peasantry to the land and stop the flight to the urban areas in pursuit of higher wages.

One such attempt was the creation of 'Hereditary Farms' (*Erbhöfe*) whereby peasants of 'German or racially similar blood' were given entailed farms of less than 125 hectares (312 acres). This amounted to a new form of serfdom in that elder sons were tied to the soil and the farm could not be sold. It did nothing to stop the movement away from the land and the number of those employed in agriculture dropped by 440,000 between 1933 and 1939. The result was a chronic shortage of farm labourers that could only be made good after 1939 by foreign labour and prisoners of war.

In spite of all these efforts the results were somewhat disappointing. Germany managed to reduce its dependence on imported foodstuffs, and there were substantial increases in the production of certain goods. Prices rose sharply and caused widespread discontent. For all the talk of 'blood and soil' it was Slav blood that worked German soil in the war years.

Extravagant promises had also been made to the middle class and they quickly saw their hopes dashed. The National Socialists had promised to break the stranglehold of the big department stores and help the struggling butchers, bakers and candlestick makers. In fact the number of small businesses declined sharply. Many were simply closed down as the economy came under ever closer state control, a process that was stepped up markedly in the latter stages of the war. Others were starved of labour. The department stores were obliged to pay higher taxes but their share of the market increased. Competition from Jewish businesses was savagely ended, and many small businessmen joined the unseemly scramble to snap up this property for bargain basement prices. But even this windfall did not offset the overall losses.

National Socialist policies towards women were also profoundly contradictory. Women were to serve the *Führer* and *Volk* by raising large numbers of children, and tending the family home rather than going out to work. On the other hand, with the increasing labour shortages women were desperately needed in the workforce.

The birth rate increased from 14.7 per thousand in 1932 to 18.6 per thousand in 1936, but this was the result of improvements in the economy rather than ideological pressure. The number of women workers increased sharply, particularly in low-paid and unskilled positions, and this in spite of generous loans offered to married women who left the workforce. Many women with university degrees were forced to quit their jobs and only a very limited number of people were admitted to institutions of higher learning. Women were weeded out of the civil service and were no longer permitted to practise law.

In spite of acute labour shortages during the war, the regime refused to introduce compulsory labour service for women. 900,000 women were forced to work in 1943, but they came from the ranks of the underprivileged. For all the talk of community, women from higher up the social scale were exempt from labour service, and Nazi Germany thus clearly remained a two-class society.

There were 3.3 million members of the National Socialist Women's Association (*Nationalsozialistische Frauenschaft* – NSF) led by the formidable Gertrud Scholtz-Klink, a slender, blonde, blue-eyed mother of six, who also was the head of the German Women's League (*Deutsches Frauenwerk* – DFW) with some 4.7 million members. In addition she was head of the women's section of the DAF. She was thus the most powerful woman in the Third Reich, but she was caught in the glaring contradiction between her vision of German women as submissive wives, mothers and housewives, and as party activists in the NSF and DFW. Scholtz-Klink was unable to find a solution to this fundamental discrepancy and her remark that the wooden spoon was as powerful a weapon as the machine-gun was somewhat unconvincing. She was further troubled by the contradiction between her prudish sexual morality and the racial theories of the party that made no distinction between legitimate and illegitimate motherhood. The regime was fundamentally antagonistic towards women in that it aimed to strengthen the role of men, and treated women as little more than breeding stock. A new law on marriage and divorce in 1938 further reduced women's legal rights.

THE FIRST STEPS IN FOREIGN POLICY

At first the regime moved very cautiously in the field of foreign affairs, and with its demands for a revision of the Treaty of Versailles it hardly distinguished itself from the other parties in Weimar Germany. Calls for the restoration of Germany's status as a great power and the return of the colonies were also commonplace in conservative and nationalist circles. But from the outset Hitler was determined to create a vast empire in eastern Europe to secure 'living space' (*Lebensraum*) and he was prepared to go to any lengths to achieve this goal. His single-minded determination, his gambler's instincts and his ruthless pursuit of long-term goals alarmed his generals and even the most robust among his myrmidons began to waver. As Hitler played for ever higher stakes and won every time his prestige grew, his critics were silenced and his charismatic status as a *Führer* of genius was further enhanced. He was thus able to manipulate the conservative nationalists and use them to help realize his vision of *Lebensraum* and the extermination of the 'racial enemies' who threatened the 'racial community'.

The international situation was very favourable for a forceful revisionist policy. The powers were seriously weakened by the Depression. Collective security was in ruins with the Japanese invasion of Manchuria and the subsequent feeble response of the League of Nations. Reparations had effectively been ended in 1932, and Brüning had got within an inch of removing the military restrictions placed on Germany by the Versailles treaty.

Hitler was anxious to allay the fears of Germany's neighbours while he established his dictatorship at home. To this end he retained the aristocratic career diplomat of the old school, Konstantin von Neurath, as foreign minister along with his secretary of state Wilhelm von Bülow. Diplomats in the Wilhelmstrasse seemed to have ignored Hitler's alarming message to his generals on 3 February 1933 and did not think that the new government meant a radical change in course. They imagined that it would be possible to pursue a somewhat more aggressive policy than that of Stresemann whereby Germany's position would be strengthened by rearmament, unification (*Anschluss*) with Austria, and the restoration of the lost colonies.

Hitler's first major public address on foreign policy was made in the Reichstag on 17 May 1933 in which he promised to respect all international treaties and obligations and called for a peaceful revision of the Versailles settlement. For all his anti-Marxist rhetoric, and while he was busy murdering communists at home, he signed a credit agreement with the Soviet Union on 25 February 1933 and a friendship and non-aggression treaty on 4 April.

On 14 October the German government took the British and French proposal at Geneva that Germany should be given a four-year trial period before reaching a general agreement on disarmament as an excuse to leave the League of Nations. This was an enormously popular move in Germany, where the League was seen as little more that an instrument whereby the victorious powers upheld the *Diktat* of Versailles.

This was followed by a surprising non-aggression pact with Poland on 16 January 1934 which marked a radical departure from the pro-Soviet and anti-Polish policy of the Weimar Republic since Rapallo. The Poles had every reason to be suspicious, particularly as Hitler pointed out that the treaty did not mean that there would be no frontier changes between the two countries, but the Poles felt abandoned by their French sponsors and believed they had no other choice.

Relations between Germany and Austria were extremely tense. Most Austrians had welcomed the idea of an *Anschluss*, but they had grave reservations now that Germany was in the hands of the National Socialists. The Austrian government complained bitterly about the massive financial help given to Austrian Nazis. The Germans replied by imposing a 1,000-mark tax on any German citizen travelling to Austria. This effectively closed the border and destroyed Austria's tourist trade. The Austrians then required visas, thus making it difficult for German Nazis to cross the border. The Austrian Nazis promptly stepped up their terror campaign that culminated in the assassination of the Chancellor Engelbert Dollfuss on 25 July 1934. Mussolini, anxious to maintain Austria as a buffer state between Italy and Germany, moved troops to the frontier and Hitler thought it prudent to disavow any connection with his unruly followers in Austria.

91 per cent of the electorate in the Saar voted in a plebiscite to return to Germany on 13 January 1935, in spite of massive anti-fascist propaganda in this largely working-class mining area. In February Hitler invited the British foreign secretary, Sir John Simon, and the Lord Privy Seal, Anthony Eden, to Berlin on 7 March to discuss an Anglo-French communiqué which proposed certain measures to avoid a renewed arms race. Then, only three days before the British delegation was due to arrive, the British government published a White Book on defence that called for substantial increases in spending on the armed forces, said to be in direct response to Hitler's overbearingly belligerent tone. Hitler, buoyed up by his remarkable victory in the Saar, promptly postponed the visit, feigning an indisposition, and took great delight in thus snubbing the British government. Six days later, on 10 March, Göring announced the formation of the *Luftwaffe*, the German air force that was expressly forbidden under the terms of the Treaty of Versailles. On 15 March the French National Assembly approved

1 *Above left:* SS – Hitler's Praetorian Guard.

2 *Above right:* SA – the brown-shirted storm troopers.

3 *Right:* An improbable hero – Horst Wessel with his brother and sister. This SA man, author of the party anthem known as the 'Horst Wessel Song', and martyr to the cause was murdered by a Communist in 1930 in an altercation over a prostitute and his failure to pay the rent.

4 The SA honouring the memory of the 'Movement's Martyr', Hans Hobelsberger, who was murdered by Communists.

5 *Gleichschaltung*: The mayor and city employees of Worms swear allegiance to Adolf Hitler.

6 1934: a class in 'Racial Studies' is introduced to the Mendelian Law of dominant and recessive characteristics.

7 Party functionaries congratulate a recipient of the 'Honour Cross of German Motherhood'; the medal was created in 1938. This woman had 'fulfilled her duty towards securing the future of the German race' by bearing more than eight children.

Ausgaben für Erbkranke – Soziale Auswirkung

Erziehungsheim in E. mit 130 Schwachsinnigen –
Ausgaben jährlich rund 104000 RM. – dafür könnte man

17 Eigenheime für erbgesunde Arbeiterfamilien erstellen

Erbkranke fallen dem Volk zur Laft

8 Euthanasia – the 104,000 marks for a home for the handicapped could have been spent to build seventeen model homes for needy workers.

9 *Above:* Anti-Semitism – the evil Jew lures two innocent Aryan children.

10 *Left:* The Eternal Jew – poster for an anti-Semitic exhibition in Munich.

11 Julius Streicher's anti-Semitic magazine on public display under the heading 'With the *Stürmer* against Jewry' and with its motto 'The Jews Are Our Misfortune', a quotation from the nineteenth-century historian Treitschke.

12 *Above:* Workers relaxing at a 'Strength Through Joy' (KdF) holiday home.

13 *Right:* Streicher's infamous anti-Semitic newspaper.

14 Shopkeepers proudly announce that theirs in a 'German Store' as part of the campaign against Jewish businesses in 1933.

15 A model working-class family in a new housing estate. The regime built 1,963,652 three- to four-room housing units between 1933 and 1939.

16 'Music While You Work': factory workers at a concert organized by 'Strength Through Joy'.

17 1939: the crowd admires the 'Strength Through Joy' (KdF) Volkswagen. In spite of all the propaganda not a single 'People's Car' was sold to the public in the Third Reich.

18 Hitler's 49th birthday present on 20 April 1938 – Ferdinand Porsche explains his invention, which was presented to the celebrant by Robert Ley. Volkswagen was part of Ley's German Work Front (DAF) empire.

19. *Left:* A 'Strength Through Joy' (KdF) cruise to the Norwegian fjords. This heavily subsidized trip cost 45 marks, all-inclusive.

20 *Right:* The Autobahn network and Volkswagen.

21 Hitler Youth take part in the 1 May celebrations in 1937.

22 A Hitler Youth band.

23 Hitler Youth at camp.

24 Members of the 'League of German Maidens' (BDM) prepare to be exemplary housewives.

25 On 1 May 1933, having destroyed the trades unions, Hitler turned their Mayday celebrations into the 'Day of National Labour'.

26 1 May celebrations in 1936.

27 Goebbels addresses a selected audience at factory in 1937.

28 *Left:* Harvest festival, October 1935. The Nazis instrumentalized all such traditional celebrations for political ends.

29 *Right:* Poster for the 1936 Olympics – they were a huge propaganda success for the Nazis.

30 1937: Swastika flags decorating the streets during the annual fish festival in Worms.

31. 'Casserole Sunday': In 1935/36 certain Sundays were designated as 'Eintopfsonntag'. 'Winter Aid' (WHW) used the 31 million marks collected from these simple meals to provide assistance for 'racially worthwhile and hereditarily healthy families' in need.

32 The Lord Mayor collecting money for 'Winter Aid'.

33 *Above:* Joachim von Ribbentrop – Hitler's foreign minister in a characteristically truculent pose.

34 *Left:* The country gentleman – Hitler at his Bavarian mountaintop retreat.

35 Goebbels inspects a model of the projected Film Academy. From left to right: Viktor Lutze (SA chief), Klitzsch (head of the state film company UFA – in SS uniform), von Lancelle (a senior official in the DAF), Professor Lehnich (President of the Reich Film Chamber).

36 *Above:* 1936: The German Army marches back into the Rhineland.

37 *Right:* January 1938 – Hitler attends Ludendorff's funeral.

38 *Above:* Preparations for war 1937: trying on the new 'peoples gas mask' provided at a cost of 5 marks.

39 *Right:* The Nazi Party's chief ideologue – Alfred Rosenberg on his 45th birthday in 1938.

40 Preparation for war 1937: collecting scrap metal to make up for the shortage of foreign currency for the import of raw materials.

41 1938: Part of the effort to prepare the nation for war.

42 Himmler addresses young Austrian Nazis after the *Anschluss*.

43 *Above:* Hitler speaks in Graz, 1938.

44 *Right:* Hitler returns in triumph to Berlin after the *Anschluss.*

45 *Below:* 18 March 1938 – Göring presides while Hitler announces elections for a new, greater German Reichstag to be held on 10 April.

46 April 1938: A storefront urging support for the *Führer* in the elections after the *Anschluss*.

Treue um Treue – dein Ja dem Führer

47 *Right:* SA men welcomed home from the Nuremberg party rally in September 1938.

48 *Below left:* Hitler drives in triumph through the streets of Cologne during the electoral campaign in 1938.

49 *Below right:* 'Tough Times, Tough Duties, Tough Hearts' – a propaganda poster from 1943.

Harte Zeiten
Harte Pflichten
Harte Herzen

an increase in the term for military service from one to two years. Then on 16 March Hitler announced the introduction of universal military service in order to create an army of 550,000 men.

Simon and Eden eventually came to Berlin on 25 March. They were treated to a series of monologues, most of them on Hitler's favourite topic of the menace of Bolshevism, and were scarcely able to get a word in edgeways. When they did manage to a register a complaint they were shot down in flames. When Sir John Simon complained of Germany's breach of the disarmament clauses of the Treaty of Versailles, Hitler enquired whether Wellington had raised similar objections when Blücher arrived on the field at Waterloo.

The French were particularly concerned with recent developments in Germany. In reaction to the Röhm putsch in June and the Austrian crisis in the following month they began fence-building with the countries in central and eastern Europe and made approaches to Moscow. The result was the Franco-Soviet mutual assistance pact of 2 May 1935, whereupon the Soviet Union joined the League of Nations. For the Soviets this was a mighty anti-fascist coalition, but it was a fissiparous alliance fraught with all manner of ideological differences and conflicts of interest. Meanwhile France's efforts to persuade Britain and Italy to stand together against German violations of the Treaty of Versailles resulted in the Stresa front of 14 April 1935 which upheld the Locarno treaty of 1925, and guaranteed the international status quo.

Hitler was not in the least bit concerned. Having clearly dominated the talks with Simon and Eden, he was convinced that if he kept up a bold front the British would be accommodating. Accordingly he sent his special representative Joachim von Ribbentrop to London to follow up on the British delegation's visit to Berlin. He reminded Paul Schmidt, Hitler's interpreter and a keen observer of human frailty, of the dog on HMV records. He was an insufferably ill-mannered former sparkling wine salesman, whose boorish behaviour soon earned him the sobriquet 'von Brickendrop'. He immediately demanded that Germany should be given a free hand in Europe to destroy the Soviet Union. In return Britannia could continue to rule the waves and concentrate on the Empire. The British government did not take kindly to this proposal to divide the world, and threatened to cancel the talks, but eventually agreed to a naval agreement on 18 June 1935 whereby the ratio of British to German surface fleets was fixed at 100 to 35. Submarines, Hitler's favoured weapon, were not included.

Hitler had every reason to consider this as his 'happiest day'. The British had single-handedly torn up the disarmament clauses of the Versailles treaty without even consulting their French allies. The British, whose eyes were on the very real threat posed by Japan, were relieved that an understanding had been reached and were determined to avoid any confrontation with Germany.

Encouraged by the feeble response of the British and French to Italy's aggression in Ethiopia, and taking the ratification of the Franco-Soviet treaty as a excuse, Hitler ordered the remilitarization of the Rhineland on 2 March 1936, having first received assurances from Mussolini that he had no serious objections to such a move. France was in the middle of an election campaign and the government was paralysed. The British did not feel that their vital interests were affected. On 7 March Hitler announced in the Reichstag that he had no further territorial demands. Eden told the House of Commons that there was no cause for alarm. Churchill's jeremiads were dismissed as the fulminations of a politician totally out of touch with the times.

Hitler's triumph in the Rhineland helped silence those who complained about the hardships caused by the concentration on rearmament and the harassment of the churches. In the elections held on 29 March 98.8 per cent voted for the '*Führer's* list'. Hitler's descent into outright megalomania was greatly accelerated by these giddy successes. His speeches were now full of references to providential guidance, his sacred mission and his visionary prescience, while Goebbels' propaganda machine pumped out clouds of adulatory incense in honour of this preternatural being.

After some initial hesitation, Hitler, prompted by ideological and economic considerations, decided to intervene in the Spanish Civil War. He now found himself fighting alongside Mussolini for General Franco's nationalists against the republicans in the 'Marxist' popular front. Mussolini had already expressed his gratitude for German neutrality over Ethiopia by ceasing to support the Austrian *Heimwehr* against the National Socialists and making it plain that he now had no objections to an *Anschluss*. The Italian foreign minister Ciano went to Berlin in October 1936 and signed a pact of mutual co-operation. He then visited Hitler in his Bavarian mountain-top retreat where his host proposed an offensive treaty designed to crush Marxism and to bring Britain to heel. Hitler said that the German army would be ready to go to war within three to five years. On 1 November Mussolini first spoke openly of an 'axis' from Rome to Berlin and invited other European states to co-operate.

Meanwhile Ribbentrop, frustrated that he had been unable to win over the British government, worked feverishly to secure an agreement with Japan so as to form a triple alliance that would leave Britain isolated. Both the German foreign office and the *Wehrmacht* leadership were opposed to the idea of a treaty with Japan, and there was considerable resistance on the Japanese side as well. Major-General Hiroshi Oshima, the military attaché who was to become ambassador later in 1936, was an enthusiastic admirer of National Socialism, and fought long and hard for an agreement with Germany. The result was the Anti-Comintern Pact of November 1936, a vague understanding that Hitler felt might help put pressure on Britain to reach an understanding with Germany.

TOWARDS THE BRINK

Rearmament was now putting an intolerable strain on the economy, military expenditure having risen from 3,300 million marks in 1933 to 9,000 million in 1936. There was a chronic shortage of foreign exchange and import prices had risen an average of 9 per cent since 1933. There was a shortage of food-stuffs resulting from a series of poor harvests, so that the regime was faced with the choice of guns or butter. Hitler was determined to keep up the pace of rearmament and therefore supported those who argued that domestic sources of raw materials should be exploited and synthetic rubber and petroleum produced so as to reduce the reliance on imports. Hitler dismissed all concerns about the horrendous cost of autarky, imagining that it would be offset by the rich booty acquired from a war of conquest. In a secret memorandum in August 1936 Hitler said that the country had to be ready for war within four years, and that a series of short campaigns would then result in an 'increase in *Lebensraum* and thus of raw materials and foodstuffs'.

Hitler gave vent to increasingly frequent outbursts about the need to find a solution to 'Germany's space question' and of the need to settle matters by force as early as 1938. On 5 November 1937 he called a top-level meeting in the chancellery attended by von Neurath, the war minister von Blomberg, as well as the commanders-in-chief of the army, the navy and the air force, von Fritsch, Raeder and Göring. They were treated to a four-hour monologue which Hitler announced should be taken as his testament in the event of his death.

It began with a rambling discourse on familiar topics such as social Darwinism, race and geopolitics, the need to strengthen the 'racial mass'

(*Volksmasse*) and to secure *Lebensraum*. None of these outstanding problems could be solved without recourse to force. He then announced that in the first stage Austria would have to be annexed, and then Czechoslovakia would be attacked. Germany would have to be prepared to fight both England and France should they decide to intervene. Hitler brushed aside all objections, but realized that he would have to replace traditionally minded men like Neurath and Fritsch to secure the co-operation of the foreign office and the army for his hazardous policy.

In January 1938 Austrian police unearthed evidence that the National Socialists were planning to cause so much disorder that the Germans would have an excuse to intervene in order to restore law and order. The Austrian Chancellor Schuschnigg decided to visit Hitler in an attempt to ease the tension between the two countries. He arrived in Berchtesgaden on 12 February 1938 and was immediately subjected to a vituperative tirade from Hitler, who accused Austria of all manner of misdemeanours including 'racial treason'. He warned the Austrian chancellor that he only had to give the order and the country would be destroyed. Ribbentrop then demanded that the National Socialist Arthur Seyss-Inquart should be put in charge of home security, that there should be a general amnesty for all Nazis, and that Austria's foreign and economic policies should be co-ordinated with the Reich. Talks between the two general staffs should also be scheduled.

Schuschnigg felt that he had no alternative but to accept, but on his return home he called for a referendum for a 'free, German, independent, social, Christian and united Austria' to be held on 13 March. The Nazis saw this as a provocation, the more so since younger voters who were highly susceptible to the movement were excluded, and Austria descended into violent anarchy. The Austrian president Wilhelm Miklas courageously refused Hitler's demand that Seyss-Inquart be appointed chancellor, whereupon the Austrian Nazis seized government buildings in Vienna. Hitler then gave orders to his troops to cross the frontier.

The German Army met with a rapturously enthusiastic welcome on 12 March, and Hitler made a triumphant return to his birthplace at Braunau before moving on to Linz where, impressed by the vast and enthusiastic crowds, he announced that Austria would be incorporated into the German Reich. From Linz he travelled to Vienna where he addressed an even larger crowd of ecstatic devotees. On 10 April a referendum was held in which 99 per cent of those eligible, including the Austrian socialist leader Karl Renner, voted in favour of the *Anschluss*. Austria promptly ceased to exist and became a German province known as the Ostmark. The

German mark replaced the Austrian shilling, and overnight Austrians had to learn to drive on the right-hand side of the road like the Germans.

For the Austrian Jewish community these were days of horror. Austrian Nazis were even more vicious and brutal in their anti-Semitism than their German comrades, and this in turn helped to radicalize the Germans immediately after the *Anschluss*. Units of the SS and police followed behind the army and, with their Austrian supporters, carried out a bestial pogrom in which thousands of innocent victims were murdered, brutally beaten, imprisoned and their property seized. Their humiliation and savage mistreatment was savoured by jeering crowds. It was a gruesome foretaste of what was to happen in Germany on 9 November.

Boosted by his triumph in Austria, encouraged by the supine attitude of Britain and France and by Mussolini's support, Hitler now turned his attention to Czechoslovakia. On 21 April he told the military that he would either go to war after a few preliminary diplomatic moves, or would use some incident to strike a lightning blow. He had already decided on the latter alternative and had instructed the Sudeten German leader Konrad Henlein to make demands of the Czechoslovakian government that could not possibly be fulfilled.

On 30 May Hitler announced that he intended 'to destroy Czechoslovakia by military means in the foreseeable future'. Throughout the summer of 1938 there was widespread violence in the Sudetenland as the crisis deepened. On 15 September the British Prime Minister Neville Chamberlain flew to Munich to meet Hitler at Berchtesgaden, and told him that neither Britain nor France would object to parts of the Sudetenland being handed over to Germany.

Hitler was caught by surprise by Chamberlain's readiness to give way and decided to take a tougher line when they met again at Bad Godesberg on 22 September. He had already told the Polish and Hungarian governments that he would support their claims against Czechoslovakia, and he now told Chamberlain that he was prepared to use force if his wishes were not immediately granted.

War now seemed inevitable. Both Czechoslovakia and France mobilized. Britain prepared for war, and the Soviet Union promised support. Hitler moved seven divisions up to the Czech border. Opposition forces in Germany went into action. General Ludwig Beck had already resigned as chief of staff in August in protest against Hitler's risky policy. Now Colonel Hans Oster, from military counter-intelligence, and the mayor of Leipzig Carl Goerdeler contacted British politicians and begged that a firm stand be taken against Hitler. Much to Hitler's disgust the majority of Germans viewed the prospect of war with sullen apprehension.

Prompted by Mussolini and by a further offer from Chamberlain, Hitler agreed to meet with the British and French prime ministers in Munich on 29 September. Without consulting either Czechoslovakia or the Soviet Union, Chamberlain and Daladier agreed that those areas in the Sudentenland where Germans were in the majority should be handed over to Germany between 1 and 10 October 1938.

In one sense Munich was a triumph for Hitler. He had gained an important industrial area, rich in natural resources and with a highly skilled labour force. Czechoslovakia was now virtually defenceless and its economy in ruins. But he had been denied the crisis that he needed were he to destroy the country and make a triumphal entry into Prague. He was furious that Chamberlain and Daladier were seen as heroes by the majority of Germans and asked: 'How can I go to war with a people like this?!' On 10 November, the day after the pogrom, Hitler gave a lengthy speech to representatives of the press ordering them to desist from all talk of peace and to steel the people for war.

On 21 October 1938 Hitler issued instructions for the destruction of Czechoslovakia and the occupation of the Memel. To this end the Slovak president Monsignor Jozef Tiso was ordered to declare Slovak independence.

Nazi Germany was now on a headlong course towards war. It was driven forward by its inner dynamics and was virtually out of control. Hitler was now an absolute dictator who paid no attention to the mounting crisis in the economy, and was impervious to all notes of caution. He talked incessantly of a 'battle of world views' and a 'racial war'. On 30 January 1939, the sixth anniversary of the 'seizure of power', he told the Reichstag: 'If international Jewry in Europe and elsewhere plunge the peoples once again into a world war, the result will not be the Bolshevization of the world, and thus a Jewish victory, but the destruction of the Jewish race in Europe.' Hitler now promised to create a vast German empire, one that was purified of all alien racial elements. There could now be no turning back.

Tiso slavishly obeyed his orders from Berlin and declared Slovak independence on 14 March. That day the Czech president Emil Hacha travelled to Berlin in a desperate attempt to preserve the independence of his rump state. Hitler ranted and raved and the unfortunate Hacha suffered a heart attack. Having been revived by Hitler's personal physician, Dr Theodor Morell, he was told that if he did not hand over the state to Nazi Germany it would be invaded. A shattered president then signed a document placing his unhappy and betrayed people 'confidently into the hands of the *Führer* of the German Reich'.

German troops crossed the frontier that night. Hitler travelled to Prague the following day to be met by a silent, crushed and tearful crowd. The Czech Republic was transformed into the 'Protectorate of Bohemia and Moravia' and was thus submitted to a pitiless occupation regime.

On 21 March German troops occupied Memel (Klaipéda), German territory that had been awarded to Lithuania under the terms of the peace treaty. This strengthened Poland's resolve to resist further German demands over the Danzig question. On 31 March the British government gave a guarantee to both Poland and Romania. Hitler was furious. On 3 April he ordered plans to be drawn up for the invasion of Poland. His 50th birthday was celebrated on 20 April with a massive military march-past in Berlin, and one week later he rescinded the Non-Aggression Pact with Poland of 1934 and the Anglo-German Naval Agreement of 1935. The next day he rejected President Roosevelt's appeal for world peace in an unrelentingly derisive speech.

Britain and France now made a somewhat half-hearted attempt to bring the Soviet Union into a European security pact, but Stalin was deeply distrustful of these two imperialist powers. Neither Poland nor Romania were at all keen to entrust their security to a power that harboured substantial claims to their territory. In May the Soviet commissar for foreign affairs, Maxim Litvinov, who was both pro-Western and Jewish, was replaced by the boot-faced Stalinist Molotov. This move was seen as a clear signal to Berlin, and was underlined by frequent mentions of Rapallo.

Hitler decided to test the water. The 'Pact of Steel' between Berlin and Rome did not amount to much, since Mussolini had made it plain that Italy would not be ready for war until 1943. Talks with Japan over a similar military alliance had come to nothing. He had set 26 August as the date for an invasion of Poland and he was virtually without an ally in this hazardous undertaking. Joachim von Ribbentrop, who had replaced von Neurath as foreign minister in 1938, made the first move towards Molotov, who reacted positively. Ribbentrop flew to Moscow on 23 August and was immediately taken to see Stalin. He thus became the first minister of a foreign government to meet Stalin. Agreement was reached within a few hours once Hitler agreed that the Soviets should be given all of Latvia. The Ribbentrop-Molotov Pact, which was in fact negotiated personally by Stalin, was a non-aggression pact to last for ten years and to become effective immediately. In a secret protocol the Soviet Union was given a free hand in eastern Poland up to the line of the Narev, Vistula and San rivers, along with Estonia, Latvia, Finland and Bessarabia (modern Moldova and western Ukraine). The future of Poland was to be settled at a later date. After the signing ceremony numerous toasts were drunk in vodka and the gangsters swapped what passed for jokes in such circles. These sordid jollifications lasted until 2 a.m.

On 25 August, the eve of the planned invasion of Poland, Hitler suffered two setbacks. The British government finally sealed the pact with Poland and Mussolini let it be known that he would not join in the war. Hitler nervously inquired whether the attack could be postponed. He was assured that it could be. 1 September was set as the new date. Göring warned Hitler that he should not play *va banque*. Hitler replied: 'I have played *va banque* my entire life!' This time there was to be no further delay. At 4.45 in the morning of 1 September the battleship *Schleswig-Holstein* opened fire on the Polish garrison on the Westerplatte by Danzig while Stuka dive-bombers swooped down on the city. Europe was once again at war.

four
THE WAR YEARS AND
THE END OF THE THIRD REICH
2 September 1939–9 May 1945

THE CAMPAIGN IN THE EAST

Britain and France declared war on 3 September, the Dominions followed suit a few days later, but they did nothing to help Poland. The 'phoney war' in the west enabled the Germans to concentrate on a swift campaign in the east. Within a week they had reached the outskirts of Warsaw. One week later the city was encircled. On 17 September the Polish government left the country and the Soviets invaded the same day. Warsaw capitulated ten days later, having been flattened by aerial and artillery bombardment. The next day Germany and the Soviet Union divided up the spoils of war. Lithuania was given to the Soviets; the Germans got Warsaw and Lublin. The fighting ended on 6 October.

SS *Einsatzgruppen* made up of men chosen from the SD and from the Security Police (*Sipo*) followed behind the victorious *Wehrmacht*. They were ordered to 'fight all elements behind the fighting troops who are enemies of the Reich and the German people'. They immediately set to work arresting 30,000 representatives of the Polish élites who were thrown into concentration camps where they were, in Heydrich's words, 'rendered harmless'. On 21 September Heydrich ordered all Jews to be herded into the larger cities. Meanwhile Himmler's order to summarily execute any *francs tireurs* was give a generous interpretation and the *Einsatzgruppen* indulged in an orgy of slaughter. They were given the enthusiastic support of those Germans living in Poland who were organized in 'self-protection' (*Selbstschutz*) units, and by units of the *Wehrmacht*. To their lasting credit and honour, some senior officers such as von Bock and Blaskowitz protested vigorously at this barbarism. Hitler dismissed their protests as 'childish' and the result of a 'Salvation Army attitude'.

In October about half of German-occupied Poland was incorporated into the Reich, the remainder was called the General Government, which was to become a reservoir of helots to serve the master race. Hitler appointed Himmler 'Reich Commissar for the Strengthening of the German Race' and he immediately set about expelling all Poles and Jews from areas recently annexed by Germany. By the end of 1940 325,000 Polish citizens had been deported, their property stolen, their place taken by Germans from the Baltic States and Volhynia.

The population was divided into four categories according to National Socialist racial criteria. At the top of the ladder came the 'citizens of the Reich' (*Reichsbürger*) made up of ethnic Germans and Poles who were deemed to be capable of being turned into Germans (*eindeutschungsfähig*). Next came two classes of 'citizens' (*Staatsangehöriger*) who were regarded as being on trial to see if they could be made into true Germans. Lastly came the 6 million Poles labelled 'protected' (*Schutzangehörigen*) who were to serve their racial superiors.

311,000 of these 'protected' Poles were shipped off to work in the armaments industry in Germany – some voluntarily, others forcibly. 400,000 further workers were sent by 1942. Meanwhile, in early 1940 the newly annexed territories were proclaimed 'free of Jews' (*Judenfrei*) and the Jews were forced into ghettos in Warsaw, Kraków, Lvov, Lublin and Radom. Large numbers of Jews were denied this temporary respite and were murdered by the *Einsatzgruppen*. The Germans were determined to exterminate the Polish intelligentsia, and 17 per cent of those listed as 'intellectuals' were murdered. Also in early 1940 the SS built a vast concentration camp at Auschwitz where Polish prisoners were treated as slave labour and executed at will. The first victims of systematic industrialized murder at Auschwitz were Soviet prisoners of war, Poles and sick inmates.

On the day that fighting stopped in Poland Hitler made a peace offer to Britain and France. It was an entirely fraudulent move for at the same time he issued orders for an invasion of Holland, Belgium and France to take place as soon as possible, insisting that he had first to have his 'hands free' in the west before taking on the Soviet Union. The military leadership felt that this was an extremely risky undertaking and the commander-in-chief Walther von Brauchitsch tried to convince Hitler to change his mind, but to no avail. Bad weather finally obliged Hitler to agree to postpone the attack on the west until 10 May 1940.

Some officers close to General Ludwig Beck plotted to overthrow Hitler. Göring again made a half-hearted attempt to stop the war because he felt that the German armed forces were not sufficiently prepared to fight what he felt was likely to be a lengthy war. A few menacing remarks by Hitler about 'defeatists' among his generals were enough to silence the opposition. Then on 9 November a cabinet maker named Georg Elser planted a bomb under the podium in the Bürgerbräukeller in Munich where Hitler addressed a meeting of 'old fighters' on the occasion of the anniversary of the 1923 coup. The bomb went off, but it missed Hitler by a few minutes.

In April 1940 the Germans invaded Norway to forestall an Anglo-French expeditionary force and to protect the Swedish ore fields which were vital to the war economy. Operation 'Weser Exercise' (*Weserübung*) was swift, economical and met with very little resistance; but the Royal Navy managed to sink a number of German ships. An attack on Denmark, 'Weser Exercise South', was an even greater success, and the whole operation was over within 24 hours.

THE CAMPAIGN IN THE WEST

Hitler's insistence on delaying the western offensive worked to Germany's advantage. Thanks to the Herculean efforts of Fritz Todt, armaments production had increased by 50 per cent, and the army now had an excellent plan based on the ideas of General Erich von Manstein. Army Group A was to drive its armour and motorized infantry through the Ardennes and then head for the Channel coast at Dunkirk in a 'sweep of the sickle'. Army Group B was to occupy Belgium and Holland and thus trap the bulk of the enemy's forces between the two Army Groups. Army Group C was to tie down the French forces in the Maginot Line without actually attacking these heavily fortified defensive positions.

The attack was launched on 10 May and went like clockwork. The French were caught off balance by the speed of the advance, the British forced to abandon the Continent in 'Operation Dynamo', a brilliantly organized evacuation. The 'Spirit of Dunkirk' became part of popular mythology and a humiliating defeat was transformed into a resounding triumph of the British spirit. The French Third Republic was riven with political dissent and began to fall apart. Armistice negotiations began on 21 June, pointedly in the same railway carriage in which the Germans had been forced to capitulate in 1918.

Characteristically the conquered territories were treated differently, thus creating a hastily improvised confusion of military, state and party administrative bodies. France was divided into the occupied northern zone and a rump state in the south with an authoritarian government in the spa town of Vichy under Marshal Pétain, the octogenarian hero of Verdun. Alsace, Lorraine and Luxembourg were annexed and ruled by *Gauleiter*. Belgium was placed under military occupation. Holland was governed by a Reich Commissar. Denmark was left as a theoretically sovereign state; its government remained in office, the Germans transmitting their requests through traditional diplomatic channels. Even though it was under military occupation it retained its own armed forces. Josef Terboven was appoint Reich Commissar for Norway who, ordered by Hitler, tried unsuccessfully to form a credible government under Vidkun Quisling, a contemptible stooge whom, like the vast of majority of Norwegians, he heartily detested.

Hitler now turned his attention to Britain. It was a frustrating problem for him. He could not understand why the British refused to make peace at a time when they appeared to be helpless. Even if Germany defeated Britain the problem of the Empire would remain. Would it fall into the hands of the Japanese or the Americans, and thus immeasurably strengthen one or even both of Germany's future rivals? Both he and his generals felt that an invasion was far too risky without first gaining absolute control over the air. To this end the Luftwaffe began massive attacks on 5 August. By switching the attacks on 24 August from airstrips and radar installations to civilian targets, the 'Few' in RAF Fighter Command were given a respite and were able to win the Battle of Britain. The air offensive was called off on 17 September and Hitler thus suffered his first serious defeat, as he himself was grudgingly forced to admit. Admiral Raeder now suggested concentrating on attacking British forces in the Mediterranean and the Middle East.

THE INVASION OF THE SOVIET UNION

On 31 July Hitler ordered his generals to prepare an attack on the Soviet Union, arguing that it was 'England's last hope'. Given that all experts agreed that the Red Army was in a state of disarray, victory was assured. Hitler said: 'We only have to kick in the front door and the whole rotten structure will collapse.' Goebbels was of the same mind: 'Bolshevism will collapse like a house of cards.' The theory that this was a preventive war fought because the Germans believed that the Soviets were about to attack is pure fantasy, behind which lurks a sinister political agenda. With virtually all of continental Europe under German control the United States would not dare to intervene. Germany would then have all the *Lebensraum* it could possibly want at its disposal.

Molotov visited Berlin on 12 and 13 November and Hitler made the preposterous suggestion that their two countries should divide up the spoils of the British Empire. Molotov replied that if Germany wished to maintain good relations with the Soviet Union it would have to agree to Soviet control over Finland, Romania, Bulgaria and the Straits, all of which were vital to the defence of the Soviet Union. Later he added Hungary, Yugoslavia and eastern Poland to this impressive list. Hitler was relieved that Molotov had provided him with further reasons for pushing ahead with plans for an attack on the Soviet Union, and announced that his pact with Stalin 'would not even remain a marriage of convenience'. On 18 December he issued 'Direction Number 21 for Case Barbarossa' which stated that 'The German Army must be ready to crush the Soviet Union in a swift campaign once the war against England is ended.'

This was to be no ordinary war. Hitler announced that it would be 'a battle between world views' in which the *Einsatzgruppen* would destroy the 'Jewish-Bolshevik intelligentsia'. No mercy was to be shown to the civilian population, Himmler and the SS were given 'special tasks' within the *Wehrmacht's* operational area involving the 'final battle between two opposing political systems'. In January 1941 Himmler announced that 30 million people in the east would have to be removed in order to ensure an adequate supply of food for Germany. This figure was increased to 31 million in the 'General Plan for the east' which Himmler published two days after the launching of Barbarossa. Hitler gave repeated instructions to the military not to treat the Red Army as normal soldiers, to ignore the rules of war and give no quarter. From the very beginning of the planning stage the *Wehrmacht* was deeply implicated in the criminal conduct of this unspeakably frightful campaign. Most of his generals enthusiastically endorsed Hitler's demented vision of a crusade against these Asiatic-Jewish-Bolshevik sub-humans. A few remained silent. None raised any serious objections.

A decree was published on 13 May to the effect that 'crimes committed by enemy civilians' did not have to go to trial and any 'suspicious elements' should be shot on the spot on an officer's orders. No German soldier was to be punished for crimes committed against enemy civilians. This was an invitation to every perverted brute and sadist to have a field day.

The infamous 'Commissar Order' was issued on 6 June whereby any Commissar captured in battle should be instantly shot. Commissars discovered behind the German lines were to be handed over to the *Einsatzgruppen* for immediate dispatch. The army objected to both these orders on practical rather than moral grounds. It was frequently argued that the Commissar Order simply strengthened Soviet determination to resist, and military discipline was severely threatened by the limitation of the Army's jurisdiction in the earlier decree.

General Georg Thomas, head of the Military Economic and Armaments Office, consulted with a number of prominent civilian officials from various ministries in the spring of 1941, and came to the conclusion that the *Wehrmacht* would have to live off the land in the Soviet Union. It was agreed that 'several million' Soviet citizens would starve to death as a result, but these worthy civil servants viewed such a prospect with equanimity.

In May Heydrich's *Einsatzgruppen* were ordered to kill all Jews in the occupied territories since they were the 'biological root' of Bolshevism. Since the *Wehrmacht* was responsible for the logistical support of the *Einsatzgruppen* once again it was deeply implicated in this indescribable crime. The much-vaunted honour of the German Army was lost forever.

In mid-December 1940 Hitler ordered preparations to be made for a campaign in the Balkans in order to secure the flank of 'Barbarossa' and to protect the Romanian oil fields from attack from the RAF. A pro-Western coup in Belgrade at the end of March 1941 enraged Hitler who ordered an immediate attack on Yugoslavia and Greece. Yugoslavia capitulated on 17 April, Greece four days later. Large numbers of German troops were now tied down in the Balkans in a brutish and bloody campaign against highly motivated and skillful partisans.

The Germans attacked the Soviet Union on 22 June 1941 with 153 divisions totalling about 3 million men. As Hitler anticipated a swift campaign lasting three months, he left few reserves at the ready, and no preparations were made for a winter campaign. The early stages of Barbarossa seemed to indicate that such confidence was justified. Within a few months Army Group North was approaching Leningrad, Army Group South had reached Kharkov and Army Group Centre began its final assault on Moscow. By mid-November the Wehrmacht was within 30 kilometres of the Soviet capital.

On 5 December Zhukov launched a massive counter-offensive, striking north and south of Moscow. The Germans were forced back some 100 to 250 kilometres and all hopes for a swift campaign were dashed. Having been locked in seemingly endless arguments with Hitler throughout the summer as to where the *Schwerpunkt* of the attack should be, Brauchitsch handed in his resignation and Hitler appointed himself commander-in-chief.

Between 22 June 1941 and March 1942 the Germans lost more than 1 million men. Only 450,000 replacements could be found. They had also lost enormous amounts of matériel and were running short of food. As early as November General Friedrich Fromm, commander of the reserve army, felt that the situation was hopeless and urged Hitler to negotiate a peace. At the same time Fritz Todt also urged Hitler to end the war given the parlous state of Germany's armaments industry. Hitler would not hear of this and entertained dark apocalyptic thoughts of a *Götterdämmerung*. 'If the German *Volk* is not strong enough and is not sufficiently prepared to offer its own blood for its existence,' he announced portentously, 'it should cease to exist and be destroyed by a stronger power.'

On 11 December Hitler declared war on the United States, four days after the attack on Pearl Harbor. It was another characteristic *va banque* play and a gesture of defiance, based on the gamble that he could win a victory in the Soviet Union before the Americans could engage in the European theatre. Referring to a speech made by Hitler on 12 December, Goebbels commented in his diary: 'This is now a world war and the annihilation of the Jews must be the necessary consequence.'

By the time the spring offensive began only 10 per cent of the wheeled vehicles lost could be made good. A mere 5 per cent of the *Wehrmacht*'s divisions were fully operational. They pushed on regardless of the fact that there was a shortage of 650,000 men, profiting from the Soviets' poor intelligence and serious operational blunders. In the summer of 1942 Army Group A of Army Group South under Hitler's direct command was ordered to head for the Black Sea and the Caucasus. The bulk of Army Group B stationed around Kursk was to push on to the Don at Voronezh and then head south-east towards Stalingrad. Paulus' Sixth Army was to break out west of Kharkov and meet up with the rest of the Army Group.

The Battle of El Alamein beginning on 23 October 1942 and the subsequent American 'Torch' landings on 8 November spelt the end of the North African campaign. On 19 November 1942 the Soviets launched a massive counter-offensive at Stalingrad that left Paulus' Sixth Army in a hopeless situation. Now nothing short of a miracle could bring victory. Hitler was so far removed from reality that his blind faith in destiny and his own unique genius was undiminished, and such was the nimbus that surrounded the 'Greatest Commander of All Time' (sometimes disrespect-fully shortened to '*Gröfaz*') that precious few grasped the true gravity of the situation.

THE SHOAH

With the invasion of the Soviet Union the Nazi persecution of the Jews entered its final and most terrible stage. When the General Government was created out of the remains of Poland, Heydrich hoped to create a 'Jewish Reservation' in the Lublin area as a temporary measure prior to a 'territorial solution' of the 'Jewish problem' somewhere in the east. This proved impractical as the area was simply not large enough, and the Jews were herded into ghettos in the larger cities. Hans Frank, the Governor of the Protectorate, also vigorously objected to the proposal, as he wanted to make his satrapy uncontaminated by Jews (*Judenrein*).

After the fall of France, Franz Rademacher, head of section III (Jewish Questions) in the foreign office, suggested that the western European Jews could be shipped off to Madagascar. Eastern Jews were considered 'more fertile, and would produce future generations versed in the Talmud and forming a Jewish intelligentsia'. They should be used as hostages so as to silence American Jews. Adolf Eichmann enthusiastically endorsed the Madagascar plan, which had long been popular in anti-Semitic circles. It was assumed that climatic conditions on the island were such that the death rate would be exceedingly high. With Britain still determined to fight on, and with the consequent shipping problem, this scheme had to be dropped.

Meanwhile conditions in the over-crowded Polish ghettos grew steadily worse, and the authorities were faced with serious problems guarding and feeding their victims. Suggestions were now made by some lower-ranking SS officers that the only solution was to kill all those who were unable to work. The situation worsened still further with the invasion of the Soviet Union with its large Jewish population. There was a conflation in the Nazi mind of Jews and partisans, as well as Jews and Bolsheviks and the Germans set about their destruction with murderous intensity. Göring, who announced that 'This is not the Second World War. This is the great racial war', gave Heydrich plenipotentiary powers on 31 July 1941 to find a 'general solution (*Gesamtlösung*) to the Jewish problem in German occupied Europe'.

In September Hitler decided that all German Jews should be expelled to the General Government. They were now forced to wear a yellow Star of

David, their few remaining civil rights were taken away from them and their property seized. Preparations were now made for the mass murder of Jews and psychiatric patients in the east so as to make room for the new arrivals. Among the first victims were those in the ghettos of Riga and Minsk as well as the psychiatric patients in the Warthegau. The *Einsatzkommandos* murdered them using carbon monoxide in mobile gas chambers, or shot them in mass executions. Extermination camps were built in Belzec, Chelmno, Sobibor and Treblinka, where gas chambers were constructed along the lines of those used to murder the handicapped in Germany in action T4, which had begun in September 1939. The gas chambers at Chelmno were first used in December 1941.

Heydrich set 9 December 1941 as the date for a major conference on 'the final solution of the Jewish question' to be held in a villa on the Wannsee in Berlin, but it had to be postponed because of the Japanese attack on Pearl Harbor.

The Wannsee conference, attended by fifteen party functionaries and senior civil servants from most of the major ministries, was eventually held at noon on 20 January 1942. Heydrich chaired the meeting and Eichmann kept the minutes. Heydrich announced his intention to render all of Europe, including Britain and Sweden, as well as North Africa, 'uncontaminated by Jews' (*Judenrein*). He estimated that a total of 11 million Jews would be deported to the east. Those who were able to work would be subject to 'natural reduction'. Those that survived would be given 'appropriate treatment' since they would otherwise represent an exceptionally tough 'germ-cell' of a Jewish revival. An exception was made for those over the age of 65 in the 'old people's ghetto' in the concentration camp in Theresienstadt. This was to serve as a model institution to counter any Allied charges of the mistreatment of Jews. Joseph Bühler, Hans Frank's deputy in the General Government, requested that the 'final solution' should begin there as soon as possible, since most of the Jews were unable to work and posed a serious economic and health problem. According to Eichmann's testimony at his trial there was a frank and open discussion of the relative merits of different methods of mass killing. The question of whether Jewish partners of 'mixed marriages' or Jewish 'half-breeds' should be deported was tabled. The meeting was brief and no objections were raised to this horrendous undertaking.

In one sense the Wannsee Conference was a confirmation of what had already been done. The decision to murder large numbers of Jews had already been taken and many of the death camps built. Hundreds of thousands had already been slaughtered in an orgy of the basest savagery, but now for the first time the intention to murder every single Jew in Europe was clearly expressed. There had been a number of previous 'final solutions to the Jewish question', but this was the definitive 'Final Solution' by means of a cold-blooded, carefully planned, industrialized and central-ized genocide, a horror unparalleled in human history.

Rudolf Höss' concentration camp at Auschwitz was now greatly expanded so as to accommodate victims from western Europe, the Balkans and the Czech Protectorate. The original camp (*Stammlager*) was now called Auschwitz I, the extermination camp at Birkenau Auschwitz II, and IG Farben's factory in the work camp at Monowitz Auschwitz III. 40,000 workers slaved away for four years in the Buna works under the most appalling conditions and all to no avail. No synthetic rubber was ever produced.

Zyklon B, a gas based on prussic acid, was first used to kill Russian prisoners of war in Auschwitz I in September 1941. The first Jews were murdered by such means in February 1942. Himmler visited Auschwitz in July 1942, witnessed the entire process from selection on the ramp to the gas chamber and crematorium, and expressed his complete satisfaction with the arrangements. He ordered a major expansion of Birkenau as a result of which up to 10,000 victims could be killed per day. Those who were not killed in the gas chambers were beaten to death, shot, were victims of ghastly medical experiments, rampant disease or malnutrition. Only the very strongest and most resourceful survived.

Well over 5 million Jews were murdered in the Shoah, but they were not the only victims of the Nazis' dystopian mania. Up to 3 million Polish Gentiles were slaughtered and at least as many Soviet civilians in addition to the 2.1 million Soviet Jews. 3.3 million Soviet prisoners of war were also killed, most of them by starvation. In addition about half a million gypsies were murdered.

The precise number of those who died in this horrific massacre will probably never be known. Precision hardly matters with figures such as these, except to counter people who deny that it ever happened, or that the number of victims was insignificant. For those who demand an accurate count Peter Witte has shown that exactly 1,274,166 Polish Jews were murdered in the gas chambers in the General Government by 31 December 1942 in the first stage of *Aktion Reinhardt*. Up to 15 million died as a result of the National Socialists' 'Racial New Order' and had they won the war the number would have been infinitely higher. In the 'General Plan for the East' prepared by the SS and published on 24 June 1941, a 'solution to the Polish question' was to follow upon the 'solution to the Jewish problem', 31 million people were to be 'resettled', a euphemism for killed, their places taken by ethnic Germans and racially suitable candidates for 'Germanization'.

The path to Auschwitz was twisted. There is no single document, verbal order, or single cause that can explain these terrible events. Every attempt to explain hardly brings us closer to an understanding and we are mindful of Carlo Levi's fellow Auschwitz inmate Iss Clausner who scratched the following words on the bottom of his soup bowl: *'Ne chercher pas à comprendre'* – 'Do not try to understand.' It needed a highly complex multiplicity of causes and actors for virulent, repulsive but still conventional anti-Semitism and racialism to result in mass murder on such an unthinkable scale. Food shortages were such that it was possible for desk-bound experts to contemplate the removal of 30 million 'useless eaters' and 'ballast material'. Housing shortages as a result of Allied bombing led to demands that Jews should be expelled from the Reich. Financial experts cast greedy eyes on Jewish property. Exotic plans were drawn up for the resettlement of eastern Europe. Half-crazed racial fanatics were free to indulge in their wildest fantasies while grim specialists on economic rationalization played with statistics and cooked up equally inhuman schemes.

The initiative did not always come from the SS. The foreign office objected to the Madagascar Plan because it was 'too slow' and would 'only' apply to Jews in occupied Europe. Thousands of anonymous accomplices were involved in a highly developed modern society in which the rule of law had broken down. Partial knowledge hardly troubled the consciences of these desktop murderers as they drew up their railway timetables, wrote their memoranda, gave their lectures on racial theory, made their films, studied the accounts, and interpreted the *Führer's* will. As the regime grew progressively more radical, all restraint was cast aside. As Goebbels said 'Whoever says A must also say B…. After a certain moment Jewish politics (*Judenpolitik*) takes on a momentum of its own.'

THE SOVIET COUNTER-OFFENSIVE

The Red Army seized the initiative in the summer of 1943 with their victory at Kursk and kept it for the rest of the war. Meanwhile the Allied landing in Sicily meant that Italy was doomed. Hitler was obliged to pull troops out of the Eastern Front to defend Italy, this at a time when the *Wehrmacht* was reeling after its defeat at Kursk. It was all in vain. Mussolini was deposed on 25 July 1943 and the Italians switched sides. By the summer of the following year the Germans had been pushed back to their starting positions on the Eastern Front in June 1941. Vichy France had been occupied as early as November 1942, three days after the Americans landed in North Africa. The successful Allied landing in Normandy on 6 June 1944 meant that Hitler's days were numbered.

The nimbus around the *Führer* began to fade as disaster followed disaster. The great gambler found himself holding a series of losing hands and nothing but a miracle could save him from ruin. For an increasing number of Germans an end to the horror now seemed preferable to what was becoming a horror without end. A small group of mostly aristocratic soldiers and civil servants now decided that the time had come to act to save Germany from total destruction and from sinking further into total moral turpitude. They were brave men who had virtually no support from the population at large, even though the regime had become savagely repressive at home and the tentacles of Himmler's SS reached every corner. Hitler became increasingly remote and isolated. Entry to the Presence was jealously guarded by his brutish secretary Martin Bormann, and he was surrounded by sycophants, court jesters and mindless agitators. The failed assassination attempt on 20 July 1944 gave this medieval despot with his warring barony a renewed popularity, and expressions of sympathy came from throughout the Reich. How could these wicked men attempt to kill the *Führer* at this moment of national peril? There was widespread approval of the bestial treatment of the conspirators, their associates and their families, who were denounced as 'reactionaries', 'toffs' and 'plutocrats' and subjected to a reign of terror. Many renewed their faith in their chiliastic saviour.

THE WARTIME ECONOMY

In spite of a series of setbacks and the devastating effects of the Allied strategic bombing campaign, armaments production peaked in the summer of 1944. This was largely the result of the exceptional efforts of Albert Speer, Hitler's young architect friend who took over responsibility for this vital sector on the death of Fritz Todt in a plane crash in February 1942. Speer struggled against Bormann, the *Gauleiter* and *Reichsleiter* to create a rationalized and centralized Ministry for Armaments and War Production that favoured large-scale production over the smaller enterprises much loved by the Nazis. Speer was only able to win the struggle because he enjoyed Hitler's full confidence.

The absurd proposition that Germany was a 'people without space', the premise on which a war to achieve *Lebensraum* had been unleashed, was soon shown to be utter nonsense. Germany was in fact a space without people, totally dependent on foreign workers. This in turn was most disturbing to strict upholders of National Socialist racial policy who had serious racial–political objections to such a policy, but who also had ideological objections to the employment of women.

Walter Darré and his 'blood and soil' disciples were deeply disturbed that by as early as 1938 a shortage of a quarter of a million agricultural workers meant that German soil was increasingly tilled by workers from the lesser breeds. By the autumn of 1944 there were about 8.5 million foreign workers in Germany, amounting to more than a quarter of the work force. The armaments industry was now dependent on foreign workers and prisoners of war. Of these about 2 million were prisoners of war, 2.8 million workers came from the Soviet Union, 1.7 million from Poland, 1.3 million from France and 600,000 from Italy. In addition there were 650,000 concentration camp inmates, most of whom were Jews.

It was easy enough to put prisoners of war to work, but few of them had the skills required in the armaments industry. The recruitment of foreigners proved exceptionally difficult, and party functionaries feared that workers from the east would weaken the 'racial basis of the biological strength of Germany', especially as there was an alarming number of instances of sexual relations between Aryan Germans and Slav sub-humans. This problem was partly overcome by moving a number of factories from Germany to the General Government. Workers from western Europe posed less of a biological threat, but it was feared that they might be prone to indulge in acts of sabotage.

In March 1942 Fritz Sauckel, the *Gauleiter* of Thuringia, was appointed General Plenipotentiary for Labour. His remit was 'to ensure the ordered employment of labour in the German war economy by taking all the measures he deems necessary in the Greater German Reich, the Protectorate, the General Government and the occupied territories.'

As a good National Socialist Sauckel refused to be bound by any legal norms. He adopted the Pauline principal of 'he who does not work shall not eat' by taking away ration books and clothing coupons from anyone who refused to work. He called this total disregard for the law 'active legit-imization'. His attempts to find volunteers by offering pay equal to that of German workers was not a success. Of 5 million foreign workers, only 200,000 came of their own accord.

Primitive living conditions, malnutrition and long working hours resulted in a noticeable decrease in productivity. Sauckel tried to overcome this by increasing wages by introducing piecework and by giving foreign workers a great deal more freedom. The result was a significant increase in productivity. Prisoners of war were not so easily bribed, and proved exceed-ingly reluctant to work for the benefit of the Greater German Reich.

All foreign workers, apart from those from Poland and the Soviet Union, were given the same wages and working conditions as Germans. They thus had paid holidays, child allowances, pension contributions and special bonuses for birthdays, marriages and deaths. Polish and Soviet workers were given the same gross wages as the others, but they were subject to special taxes which left them between 10 and 17 marks per week. Since they had to pay 1.50 marks per diem for board and lodging, they were left with little over at the end of the week. Progressive taxation was so steep that no amount of overtime made any significant different in net wages.

Sauckel reduced the burden on taxation of Soviet and Polish workers significantly. He also allowed Polish workers to travel home until shortage of transportation made this impossible. Soviet workers were not permitted to travel, but were given a few days' rest provided they could be spared from work.

Sauckel soon found himself in direct conflict with the SS. He was anxious to find as many able-bodied workers as possible, and therefore insisted that they should be properly fed, housed and clothed, and given adequate incentives to work. The SS aimed to kill all the millions of Soviet prisoners of war along with the hundreds of thousands of Jews who were working for the Germans. The SS won the struggle, and millions of Soviet prisoners of war were worked until they dropped or starved to death.

In the final stages of the war the situation of foreign workers and prisoners of war became desperate. They wandered among the rubble of the ruined cities in search of food and shelter. Many organized themselves into armed bands and had pitched battles with the security forces. Those caught plundering, in other words those who actually found something to eat, were shot on the spot. 200 Soviet citizens were shot in Dortmund, and in Suttrop in the Sauerland 129 men, 77 women and two small children were murdered on the order of SS General Kammler. At Arnsburg in

Hessen the SS men who refused to execute a group of Soviet women lie buried beside them amid the ruins of a beautiful Cistercian monastery. Their sacrifice is a reminder that amid these unimaginable horrors human decency and extraordinary moral courage was never wholly absent, often appearing in the most surprising places.

DEFEAT

On 16 December 1944 the last German offensive was launched in the Ardennes against the American forces in Luxembourg and Belgium. It was a pale imitation of 'Plan Yellow' of 1940 and further weakened the hard-pressed Eastern Front. The Americans were at first caught completely by surprise, but reserves were rushed in to halt the German advance. Brigadier-General McAuliffe stopped von Manteuffel's Fifth Panzer Army at Bastogne, and to the south Patton's Third Army made a brilliant 90-degree shift north to hit the southern flank of the 'Bulge'. The ill-equipped and exhausted Germans fought tenaciously with inadequate air cover and relying solely on Allied fuel depots for replenishments. The odds against them were overwhelming. The Allies launched their counter-offensive on 3 January and within a few days it was clear that Hitler's final *va banque* had failed. He had expended his slender reserves that were badly needed to meet the Soviet winter offensive, which began on 12 January, and the *Luftwaffe* virtually ceased to exist.

Hitler returned to Berlin on 16 January, spending the rest of his days huddled with his cronies in the bunker under the chancellery where the atmosphere was claustrophobic, divorced from reality and nightmarishly apocalyptic. Meanwhile, millions of half-starved refugees trudged westwards to escape the Red Army, which indulged in a disgusting orgy of murder, rape, plunder and mass deportations to the Gulag. Poles and Czechs joined in this appalling debauch, taking terrible revenge on their oppressors. Hundreds of thousands of Germans who suffered from this barbaric treatment must also be counted among the millions of Hitler's innocent victims.

Hitler took to the airwaves for the last time on 30 January to give his traditional address on the anniversary of the 'seizure of power'. It was a poor performance full of talk of fighting to the death against 'Asiatic Bolshevism', but it was clear to all around him that the war was lost. On 15 March 1945 Speer pointed out that the war economy had collapsed not because of Allied bombing, but because of the loss of essential sources of raw materials, particularly Romanian oil, and because of the destruction of the transportation network. The Allies would soon be in the Ruhr and it was thus pointless to prolong the war. In fact it was Allied bombers that had effectively disrupted transport and they now concentrated on the destruction of oil refineries, bridges, canals and chemical plants.

Allied bombing resulted in about 600,000 deaths and destroyed 3.37 million homes. It obliged the Germans to employ 800,000 people in air defence; other fronts were thus denuded of artillery, aircraft and manpower. There was a desperate shortage of aluminium resulting from its use in fuses for anti-aircraft shells. It clearly had a devastating effect on civilian morale, and there was widespread disillusionment with a leadership that failed so spectacularly to defend the fatherland. The morality of strategic bombing is questionable, but attempts by some to make men like 'Bomber' Harris the moral equivalents of Heinrich Himmler are clearly grotesque.

Hitler ignored Speer's pleading that the German people had to be left with some means of subsistence in the post-war world, and argued that a people who had shown themselves so weak and feeble deserved to be destroyed. To his dismay Germany's performance in this titanic clash between the races had demonstrated that his lunatic vision of the biological-racial superiority of the German *Volk* was woefully deficient. On 19 March he issued his 'Nero Order' calling for the total destruction of Germany's economy. Mercifully this insane command was seldom obeyed. The *Führer's* wish was no longer law.

Hitler's 56th birthday on 20 April was a gloomy affair during which he decided he would stay in Berlin to the last. On 29 April he married his long-term and long-suffering mistress, Eva Braun. He then dictated his political testament. Even his devoted secretary Traudl Junge was appalled by this mean-spirited and repulsive document. Hitler and his young bride committed suicide the following day at 3.30 p.m.

Meanwhile, on 23 April Göring, who had removed himself to Berchtesgaden, asked whether he could take over command, as Hitler no longer had any freedom of action. Hitler's reply was to dismiss him from the party. Himmler sent out some peace feelers whereupon Hitler ordered his arrest. The *Reichsführer*-SS ended his wretched life with a cyanide pill on 23 May. Goebbels failed in an attempt to sign a separate peace with the Soviets and committed suicide along with his wife on 1 May, having first murdered their six children.

On 6 May Jodl signed an act of surrender at Reims. The laconic General Eisenhower reported to the Combined Chiefs that the Allied mission was over. On 9 May Keitel signed a second act of surrender along with Marshal Zhukov and Air Marshal Tedder in Berlin and Hitler's war was thus formally ended.

It was also the end of National Socialism. The Third Reich left nothing behind it but horror. The horror of tens of millions of dead, of a continent laid waste, the horror of a great nation reduced to barbarism, moral squalor and mass murder, soon to be crippled by guilt. It is a horror that will not go away, that refuses to distance itself by becoming history; it is the horror of the unfathomable.

SELECT BIBLIOGRAPHY

GENERAL WORKS

Bracher, Karl-Dietrich, *The German Dictatorship*, London 1970. An older but still useful survey.

Burleigh, Michael, *The Third Reich*, New York 2000. An immensely detailed recent study that revives the theory of totalitarianism and sees National Socialism as a form of political religion.

Hiden, John, and John Farquharson, *Explaining Hitler's Germany*, London 1989. A lively discussion of different approaches to the problem of National Socialism.

Hildebrand, Klaus, *The Third Reich*, London 1984. A brief but helpful guide.

Kershaw, Ian, *The Nazi Dictatorship*, London 1995. A valuable discussion of the literature on the Third Reich.

Noakes, Jeremy, and Geoffrey Pridham (eds), *Nazism, 1919-1945. A Documentary Reader*, Exeter 1983-98. An invaluable collection of key documents.

BIOGRAPHIES OF HITLER

Bullock, Alan, *Hitler. A Study in Tyranny*, London 1964. The first serious biography of Hitler and still well worth reading.

Fest, Joachim, *Hitler*, London 1974. A superbly written account.

Kershaw, Ian, *Hitler 1889-1936. Hubris*, London 1998

Kershaw, Ian, *Hitler 1936-1945. Nemesis*, London 2000. The latest, most detailed and best biography.

ASPECTS OF THE DICTATORSHIP

Balfour, Michael, *Withstanding Hitler in Germany 1933-1945*, London 1988. An excellent overview of the resistance.

Barkai, Avraham, *From Boycott to Annihilation. The Economic Struggle of German Jews 1933-1945*, Brandeis 1989. A well-researched account of the economic aspects of the persecution of German Jews.

Barkai, Avraham, *Nazi Economics. Ideology, Theory and Policy*, Oxford 1990. A fascinating account of an important and often overlooked aspect of National Socialism.

Bergen, Doris L., *Twisted Cross. The German Christian Movement in the Third Reich*, Chapel Hill 1996. A beautifully written and superbly researched study of the 'German Christians'.

Burleigh, Michael, and Wolfgang Wippermann, *The Racial State. Germany 1933-1945*, Cambridge 1991. A helpful analysis of Nazi racial theory and practice.

Burleigh, Michael, *Death and Deliverance. Euthanasia in Germany c.1900-1945*, Cambridge 1994. A powerful account of the euthanasia programme.

Conway, J.S., *The Nazi Persecution of the Churches 1933-1945*, London 1968. An older but still unsurpassed survey of Nazi policies towards the churches.

Deist, Wilhelm, *The Wehrmacht and German Rearmament*, London 1981. A concise and definitive account by an acknowledged expert.

Evans, Richard J., *The Coming of the Third Reich*, London 2004. The magisterial first volume of what will be the definite history of the Third Reich.

Farquharson, J.E., *The Plough and the Swastika. The NSDAP and Agriculture in Germany 1928-1945*, London 1976. The best study of the 'blood and soil' policy.

Friedländer, Saul, *Nazi Germany and the Jews. The Years of Persecution 1933-1939*, London 1998. An excellent survey of this harrowing topic.

Gellately, Robert, *The Gestapo and German Society*, Oxford 1988. A remarkable local study that shows how the effectiveness of the Gestapo depended on the active support of the citizenry.

Graml, Hermann, *Anti-Semitism in the Third Reich*, Oxford 1992. A balanced and succinct account of a complex problem.

Hoffmann, Peter, *The History of German Resistance to Hitler 1933-1945,* Montreal 1996. The definitive work on the resistance.

James, Harold, *The German Slump. Politics and Economics 1924-1936*, Oxford 1986. An accessible account of a complex problem.

Kershaw, Ian, *The 'Hitler Myth'. Image and Reality in the Third Reich,* Oxford 1987. A thoughtful study of Hitler's leadership in theory and practice.

Klemperer, Viktor, *I Shall Bear Witness. The Diaries of Viktor Klemperer*, London 1998-9. A shattering and detailed account of everyday life in the Third Reich. Essential reading.

Koonz, Claudia, *Mothers in the Fatherland*, New York 1988. A brilliant study of Nazi attitudes to women and motherhood.

Müller, Klaus-Jürgen, *The Army, Politics and Society in Germany 1933-1939*, Manchester 1987. The best study of the role of the Army in peacetime.

Nekrich, Aleksandr M., *Pariahs, Partners, Predators. German-Soviet Relations 1922-1941*, New York 1997. A thought-provoking study of German-Soviet relations prior to Barbarossa.

Overy, Richard J., *Göring. The Iron Man*, London 1983. Highly readable and reliable account of one of the key figures in the Third Reich.

Overy, Richard J., *The Nazi Economic Recovery, 1932-1938*, Cambridge 1996. An invaluable and straightforward discussion of an often debated subject.

Paucker, Arnold, *Jewish Resistance in Germany. The Facts and the Problems*, Berlin 1991. A stimulating account of an often overlooked question.

ASPECTS OF HITLER'S WAR

Glantz, David M., Barbarossa. *Hitler's Invasion of Russia 1941,* Stroud 2001. The best short account of the campaign.

Gorodetsky, Gabriel, *Grand Delusion. Stalin and the German Invasion of Russia*, New Haven and London 1999. A meticulously researched and brilliantly argued study of Nazi-Soviet relations on the eve of Barbarossa.

Grossmann, Vasily, *Life and Fate*, London 1985. A masterly novel that analyses the Battle of Stalingrad from both sides.

Herbert, Ulrich, *Hitler's Foreign Workers. Enforced Foreign Labour in Germany under the Third Reich*, Cambridge 1997. A nuanced study of a key issue.

Kitchen, Martin, *Nazi Germany at War*, New York 1995. An overview of various aspects of life on the home front.

Mulligan, Timothy, *The Politics of Illusion and Empire. German Occupation Policy in the Soviet Union 1942-43*, New York 1988. A helpful introduction to a grim topic.

Overy, Richard J., *Russia's War*, London 1997. A brilliant account of how Hitler lost the war.

Overy, Richard J., *The Air War, 1939-1945*, London 1980. A robust account of the Allied bombing campaign that has withstood recent attacks.

Overy, Richard J., *Why the Allies Won*, London 1995. Essential reading for an understanding of the war.

THE SHOAH

Arad, Yitzak, Shmuel Krakowski, and Shmuel Spector (eds), *The Einsatzgruppen Reports*, New York 1989. Reports from the SS murder-squads in the east.

Arad, Yitzak, Yisrael Gutman and Abraham Margaliot (eds), *Documents of the Holocaust*, Jerusalem 1981. A useful collection of key documents.

Bauer, Yehuda, *The Holocaust in Historical Perspective*, London 1978. An earlier analysis of the literature on the Holocaust.

Benz, Wolfgang, *The Holocaust*, New York 1999. A concise and balanced account by a leading expert.

Breitmann, Richard, *The Architect of Genocide. Heinrich Himmler and the Final Solution*, London 1991. A useful and readable biography.

Browning, Christopher, *Paths to Genocide*, Cambridge 1994. Stimulating studies on various aspects of the Holocaust.

Browning, Christopher, *Ordinary Men. Reserve Battalion 101 and the Final Solution in Poland*, New York 1993. A lively and much-discussed study of men reduced to barbarism.

Hilberg, Raul, *The Destruction of the European Jews*, New York 1983. The first, updated and classic account that remains essential reading.

Longerich, Peter, *The Unwritten Order: Hitler's Role in the Final Solution*, Stroud 2001. The best study of a much-debated question.

Marrus, Michael, and Robert Paxton, *Vichy France and the Jews*, New York 1983. A milestone study of an issue that had been shamefully overlooked.

Marrus, Michael, *The Holocaust in History*, London 1989. An excellent account of the literature on the Holocaust.

Trunk, Isaiah, *Judenrat. The Jewish Councils in Eastern Europe under Nazi Occupation*, New York 1972. A vigorous discussion of Jewish responses to a deadly threat.

LIST OF ILLUSTRATIONS

Images credited 'Bönnen' are photographs by Leopold Hanselmann (1900–1942), reproduced from Gerold Bönnen, Worms: Fotos von Leo Hanselmann, Sutton Verlag 2000. Images with no credit are supplied by the author.

25 On 1 May 1933, having destroyed the trades unions, Hitler turned their Mayday celebrations into the 'Day of National Labour'. (Bönnen)

26 1 May celebrations in 1936. (Bönnen)

27 Goebbels addresses a selected audience at factory in 1937.(Bönnen)

28 Harvest festival, October 1935. (Bönnen)

29 Poster for the 1936 Olympics.

30 1937: Swastika flags decorating the streets during the annual fish festival in Worms. (Bönnen)

31 'Stew Sunday': In 1935/36 certain Sundays were designated as 'Eintopfsonntag'. (Bönnen)

32 The Lord Mayor collecting money for 'Winter Aid'. (Bönnen)

33 Joachim von Ribbentrop.

34 The country gentleman – Hitler at his Bavarian mountaintop retreat.

35 Goebbels inspects a model of the projected Film Academy.

36 1936: The German Army marches back into the Rhineland. (Bönnen)

37 January 1938 – Hitler attends Ludendorff's funeral.

38 Trying on the new 'people's gas mask' provided at a cost of 5 marks. (Bönnen)

39 Alfred Rosenberg on his 45th birthday in 1938.

40 Collecting scrap metal to make up for the shortage of foreign currency for the import of raw materials. (Bönnen)

41 1938: Part of the effort to prepare the nation for war. (Bönnen)

42 Himmler addresses young Austrian Nazis after the *Anschluss*.

43 Hitler speaks in Graz, 1938.

44 Hitler returns in triumph to Berlin after the *Anschluss*.

45 Göring presides while Hitler announces elections for a new, greater German Reichstag.

46 A storefront urging support for the *Führer* in the elections after the *Anschluss*. (Bönnen)

47 SA men welcomed home from the Nuremberg party rally in September 1938. (Bönnen)

48 Hitler drives in triumph through the streets of Cologne during the electoral campaign in 1938.

49 'Tough Times, Tough Duties, Tough Hearts' – a propaganda poster from 1943.

INDEX

If you are interested in purchasing other books published by Tempus,
case you have difficulty finding any Tempus books in your local bookshop,
you can also place orders directly through our website

www.tempus-publishing.com